Bridging Our Faiths

Prepared by

The Interreligious Council of San Diego

in conjunction with

The National Conference

Paulist Press
New York/Mahwah, N.J.

Acknowledgments

The Publisher gratefully acknowledges use of the following materials: A photograph of "Muslims praying in the upper gallery of the main mosque in the old walled city on the occasion of Eid al-Fitr, which celebrates the end of the holy fasting month of Ramadan," and a photograph of "Indian women carrying pitchers containing holy water of the river Ganges, beginning of a grand Hindu religious ritual 'Ashwamedh Yajna.'" Both photographs were reprinted with permission from Reuters/Corbis-Bettmann.

Cover design by Cindy Dunne

Book design by Saija Autrand/Faces Type & Design

ISBN: 0-8091-9574-7

Published by Paulist Press
997 Macarthur Boulevard
Mahwah, New Jersey 07430

Printed and bound in the
United States of America

Contents

Introduction

In response to a request from the San Diego city schools, the Interreligious Council of San Diego created this volume as a supplement for middle and high school social studies classes on topics of religion omitted from the standard textbooks. It is for use as a religion text in the classrooms of any public or private school, with the explanation of the different faiths provided by the members of those faiths themselves.

As the Superintendent of Schools for San Diego says so well in her letter of appreciation to the Council:

"I thank the council for their efforts, and for this excellent contribution to the district's social studies program.

As stated in the *Moral and Civic Education and Teaching About Religion* handbook, adopted by the State Department of Education, 'Students should comprehend the religious ideas that have helped to shape Western and Eastern cultures and civilizations; they should become aware of the influence of religion on life-styles (work, prayer, devotion, ritual, worship, meditation) and on the development of ideas.' The teacher's challenge is to teach about world religions in the historical context and to ensure that objectivity, fairness, and sensitivity be evident in the process.

We are indeed fortunate that a group of religious community leaders had the foresight and expertise to write this supplement. The Interreligious Council, convened by the San Diego National Conference, has filled a critical need by expanding and clarifying issues central to the responsible teaching of religion in the classroom.

Prior to the district's adoption of the Houghton Mifflin textbooks on March 11, 1992, very little had been written about world religions in social studies textbooks. How can we, as a society, have better understanding of our cultural diversity if we do not make attempts to study and understand other peoples' religions? My hope is that the current textbooks, with this supplement, will help students and teachers better understand and accept the wonderful diversity of people who live in our community and the world."

Bertha O. Pendleton
Superintendent of Schools

Foreword

This text was initially prepared by the Interreligious Council of San Diego in response to a request from the San Diego Unified School District to develop a body of work, appropriate for student use, that would accurately portray the core beliefs of traditional and emerging faith communities.

As the racial and ethnic diversity of our nation's population continues to increase, so does its religious diversity. Absent efforts to challenge the misconceptions and stereotypes that "the stranger" engenders, bias bigotry, prejudice and even violence will continue to characterize relationships among and between communities of faith.

Protestants and Catholics continue their violent struggles in Northern Ireland; Muslims and Christians war in Bosnia, members of the Bahá'í faith continue to be persecuted in Iran, and the Middle East remains a quagmire. Here in the United States churches are still burned, mosques are threatened with bombings, and swastikas still deface temples and synagogues.

If we are to increase our understanding of and respect for one another's spiritual traditions and reduce the real and perceived animosities of one faith community toward another, it is time to demonstrate our openness to sharing who we are and what we value. *Bridging Our Faiths* is one such effort.

Unlike traditional comparative religion texts, each section of this book was written by members of the faith community described. There has been no censorship of materials. All of the materials are presented in a manner that provides an historic context for each tradition; none of the text attempts to proselytize. The reader will note that some faith traditions are presented more comprehensively than others. This is based on the author's decision that there are many more historically accurate materials about some faiths than others and therefore lesser known traditions are presented in greater depth. The authors accept responsibility for this decision.

The Interreligious Council recognizes that some spiritual traditions are not represented in the text. Invitations to a number of faith communities were extended and were either declined or unanswered. The Council further recognizes that within some faith traditions presented there is a diversity of perspective and practice and that the text may present some but not all views of a particular faith community. This is noted where appropriate.

The Interreligious Council of San Diego was established by The National Conference (founded as The National Conference of Christians and Jews) in 1991 to promote mutual understanding and respect among faith communities. Council members acknowledge the differences among their respective faiths but celebrate their many shared interests and values. The Council values religious, cultural and ethnic diversity yet is acutely aware of the dangers that result from ignorance and misunderstanding about our respective beliefs, customs and ancestries. It is our hope that *Bridging Our Faiths* will be a useful resource in the journey of understanding and acceptance.

Carol Rogoff Hallstrom, Regional Director
The National Conference
San Diego, California

FOUNDING MEMBERS
INTERRELIGIOUS COUNCIL
OF SAN DIEGO

Bahá'í Faith

Roman Catholic Diocese

Buddhist Temple of San Diego

Ecumenical Council of San Diego

Islamic Services Foundation

San Diego Rabbinical Association

Vedanta Society of Southern California

Convened by

The National Conference

Contributors to
Bridging Our Faiths
are:

Swami Atmarupananda

Imam Sharif Battikhi

Susan Collins, A.B., M.A.

Margaret Hough

Keith Christian Jensen, Ph.D.

Rabbi Martin S. Lawson

Rev. Nancy McMaster, M. Div

Rev. Dennis L. Mikulanis, S.T.D.

Rev. Akio Miyaji

Rabbi Leonard Rosenthal

Jane Senour, A.B., M.S., M.A.

Abdussatar Shaikh, Ph.D.

Thomas Shanks, A.B., M.A., MPH

Robert Stockman, Ph.D.

Bahá'í Faith

Prayer for Youth

O Lord! Make this youth radiant and confer Thy bounty upon this poor creature. Bestow upon him knowledge, grant him added strength at the break of every morn and guard him within the shelter of Thy protection so that he may be freed from error, may devote himself to the service of Thy Cause, may guide the wayward, lead the hapless, free the captives and awaken the heedless, that all may be blessed with Thy remembrance and praise. Thou art the Mighty and the Powerful.

—Abdu'l Bahá

"The present conditions of the world—its economic instability, social dissension, political dissatisfaction and international distrust—should awaken the youth from their slumber and make them inquire what the future is going to bring. It is surely they who will suffer most if some calamity sweeps over the world. They should therefore open their eyes to the existing conditions, study the evil forces that are at play and then with a concerted effort arise and bring about the necessary reforms— reforms that shall contain within their scope the spiritual as well as social and political phases of human life."

*A letter written on behalf of
the Guardian Shoghi Effendi*

Seat of the International Governing Body

Shrine of the Bab, Mt. Carmel

International Bahá'í Archives

Scenes of Mt. Carmel. Bahá'í World Center. Haifa, Israel.

INTRODUCTION AND BASIC TENETS

The Bahá'í Faith is a religion that was founded in Persia (now called Iran) in the middle of the nineteenth century. It teaches that all people of the world are members of one human family. It also teaches that all religions are basically the same and that all religions worship the same God. According to the Bahá'í Faith, one day all the countries of the world will join together as one country with one religion.

The founder of the Bahá'í Faith was called Bahá'u'lláh. He taught that all the great religions of the world are divine in origin, that their basic principles are in complete harmony, that their aims and purposes are the same, and that their teachings are aspects of one truth. He explained that a Messenger from God is sent about once every 1,000 years to provide spiritual guidance to humankind in a continuous and progressive process. Their missions represent successive stages in the spiritual evolution of human society. The unity and oneness of humankind is the central point of the Bahá'í Faith, and the point from which all of its other teachings grow.

The Bahá'í Faith is the second most widely disseminated religion in the world, and one of the fastest growing. Its central religious figures are the Báb (1819–1850), a Messenger of God and the Herald of the Great World Redeemer; Bahá'u'lláh (1817–1892), the founder of the Bahá'í Faith and the Divine Messenger of God for the present age; and 'Abdu'l-Bahá (1844–1921), Bahá'u'lláh's oldest son, His appointed successor and the interpreter of His writings.

Pronunciation Guide

Báb	Bob	"Door" or "Gate"
Bábí	Bob-ee	Follower of the Báb
Bahá'í	Bah-HIGH or Bah-Hah-ee	Follower of Bahá
Bahá'u'lláh	Bah-Hah-oo-lah	Glory of God
'Abdu'l-Bahá	Ab-DUL-Ba-HA	Servant of Bahá
Shoghi Effendi	SHOW-ghee-eFEN-dee	'Abdu'l-Bahá's grandson

Bahá'ís believe in

- **the oneness of humanity**. All people are members of the human family, all have the same Creator.

- **the independent investigation of truth**. Bahá'u'lláh teaches that each person must investigate truth for himself—that faith in this day must be built on knowledge and based on one's own decision.

- **elimination of all prejudices**. For example, gender, religion, age, nationality, racial, economic, appearance, cultural.

- **agreement of science and religion**. Bahá'u'lláh teaches that true religion and true science are in complete harmony.

- **world peace**. This is the time when all nations must seek, by every means in their power, to establish cooperation of all the nations and the world.

- **equality of men and women**. Both men and women are equal in the sight of God and both should have the same rights and responsibilities.

- **universal education**. Everyone, rich and poor, men and women, should receive an education.

- **consultation**. Truth and the best decisions emerge from a process of honest and open discussion by every member of a group.

- **limitation of wealth and poverty**. Society must not permit extremes of either wealth or poverty. The economic problem is essentially a spiritual one.

- **universal language**. Bahá'u'lláh recommended the adoption of a common second language for all peoples in order to promote greater understanding between nations and individuals.

- **unity in diversity.** The different languages and cultures of the world should maintain their individuality, but there must be a common link between them that can bring about understanding.

- **a world commonwealth of nations.** This is the time when the peoples of the earth should meet as equals. Their governments will be represented in a world parliament that will be concerned with the prosperity of all nations and the happiness of humankind.

- **progressive revelation.** God has unfolded divine truth in successive stages through the whole history of humankind. This means that religion is evolutionary—it develops and progresses over the ages. Bahá'u'lláh's divine mission is to unite humankind into one global Faith.

History of the Bahá'í Faith

The Báb. From 1844 to 1850, the religion was led by Mirza' Ali Muhammad, who became known to His followers as the Báb. This means the gate, as many people saw Him as the gateway to a new truth. Many people in Persia were impressed by the Báb's teachings and His message quickly spread. However, some of the political and religious leaders hated and feared the Báb, because their wealth and power were threatened by His teachings. They tried to end His preaching and influence by imprisoning Him, but more and more people began to believe in His message. The Báb was executed in Persia on July 9, 1850. Thousands of His followers died in the persecution that followed.

Bahá'u'lláh. An important part of the Báb's teaching concerned His prophecy that another and greater prophet would come after Him. In 1863, a follower of the Báb named Mírzá Husayn'Ali declared that He was the long expected Teacher and Educator of all peoples. He became the head of the new religion and became known as Bahá'u'lláh, which means *Glory of God*. The word *Bahá'í* means *follower of Bahá'u'lláh*.

Bahá'u'lláh brought many new teachings and prayers to His followers. He also revealed new social laws of Bahá'ís. Although Bahá'u'lláh's teachings promoted world peace, He and His family were prisoners for the rest of His life, and were exiled to many countries. His final home was in the prison city of Akka in Palestine, which is now part of Israel.

Bahá'u'lláh revealed more than 100 religious works, including the "Kitab-i-Aqdas" (The Most Holy Book). He said the world was paying too much attention to war and not enough attention to religion. He taught that people should turn toward God, and join together to bring peace to the world. He wrote letters to kings, rulers and heads of religions, asking them to meet and agree to stop war. Bahá'u'lláh died in 1892 in Israel. The shrine where He is buried and the homes where He was a prisoner are now Bahá'í Holy places, visited by Bahá'ís.

'**Abdu'l-Bahá**. When Bahá'u'lláh died in 1892, He provided for the future development of the religion in His will. The will named His oldest son 'Abdu'l-Bahá as the Interpreter of the Bahá'í teachings. From 1892 until he died in 1921, 'Abdu'l-Bahá provided leadership to the Bahá'ís. He brought the faith to more than 30 countries around the world by traveling and sending out Bahá'í teachers. He also wrote books that deal with questions about religion, peace, and society.

Between 1911 and 1913 'Abdu'l-Bahá traveled in Europe, Canada, and the United States, asking the nations, races, and religions to unite for the sake of peace. He encouraged the American Bahá'í community, which was beginning to develop. One place he met with Bahá'ís was in Wilmette, Illinois, near Chicago, on land where Bahá'ís planned to build a House of Worship. This building was opened for public worship in 1953. It has become well known for its beautiful and unusual style of architecture. Before his death in 1921, 'Abdu'l-Bahá appointed a new Guardian of the Faith, his grandson Shoghi Effendi (1897-1957), who directed Bahá'í activities until his death in 1957.

Universal House of Justice. In 1963, following the guidelines of Bahá'u'lláh, the Universal House of Justice was elected as the main administrative body. Today Bahá'ís live under the guidance and protection of this body of nine Bahá'ís, newly elected every five years. The world headquarters are located in Haifa, Israel, on Mount Carmel. The Bahá'í World Center includes the Seat of the Universal House of Justice, The Shrine of the Báb, an archives building, many office buildings, and beautiful gardens.

The Bahá'í Faith has spread to more than 200 countries and dependencies. There are National Spiritual Assemblies in 170 countries and territories. Literature of the faith is published in 800 languages. In addition to the temple in Wilmette, Bahá'í houses of worship have been built in Kampala, Uganda; Sydney, Australia; Panama City, Panama; Frankfurt, Germany; Samoa; and New Delhi, India.

The Bahá'ís have no ministers or priests. Their meetings are for worship and spiritual education. Their activities are directed by elected bodies known as Spiritual Assemblies. Every Bahá'í should pray daily and study the sacred writings. Adults fast for 19 days a year, during the Bahá'í month of Ala, going without food from sunrise to sunset. Alcohol and non-medical drugs are forbidden. The Bahá'í calendar has 19 months of 19 days with 4 extra days (5 days in a leap year). The year begins on March 21, the first day of spring.

ANSWERS TO QUESTIONS

1. What defines affiliation with your religious tradition?

Bahá'u'lláh teaches that each person must investigate truth for himself or herself without relying on someone else's thinking. Someone wishing to become a Bahá'í signs a declaration card acknowledging belief in Bahá'u'lláh as the Promised One of God. Fifteen is the age at which a child attains spiritual maturity. Children of Bahá'í parents are considered to be Bahá'ís until they are 15, after which they may formally affirm their faith in Bahá'u'lláh.

2. What are the rituals of your tradition that surround the rites of passage?

The Bahá'í Faith does not have ritual observances that must be adhered to. Individuals plan observances which include the reading of Bahá'í Holy Writings.

Those areas of Bahá'í life that are most subject to regulations are marriage, divorce, death and burial, certain aspects of lifestyle, and membership in certain non-Bahá'í organizations. Marriage requires consent of both parties and their parents; divorce is permitted but discouraged. Apart from marriage and burial, there is no formal commemoration of the main passages of life (birth and the attainment of religious and legal maturity), nor is entry into the Bahá'í community normally marked by any special ceremony. Individuals are free to observe these events as they wish.

3. What are the major holidays within your religious tradition, and what does each represent?

The Bahá'í calendar contains a year of 19 months, each with 19 days. There are also four or five intercalary days to bring the Bahá'í year into alignment with the solar year. There are 11 Holy Days (underlines indicate days when Bahá'ís should not work):

• *Naw-Rúz,* The New Year	March 21
• Ridván Festival, Bahá'u'lláh's declaration of His mission	
1st day	April 21
9th day	April 29
12th day	May 2
Declaration of the Báb	May 23
Ascension of Bahá'u'lláh	May 29
the date of Bahá'u'lláh's death	
• *Martyrdom of the Báb*	July 9
the date the Báb was executed for His religious belief	
• *Birth of the Báb*	October 12
• *Birth of Bahá'u'lláh*	November 12

- Day of the Covenant   November 26
- Ascension of 'Abdu'l-Bahá   November 28
  The date of the death of
  'Abdu'l-Bahá
- Ayyám-i-Há (Intercalary Days)   February 25-March 1
  Special time of fellowship and
  parties, gift giving, and acts of
  service to others
- Period of fasting   March 2-March 20

4. Does your tradition have a view of an afterlife and, if so, describe it briefly.

Bahá'ís believe that the experience we call death leads to a life immeasurably richer and more beautiful than we can ever imagine in this world. We should prepare for it and look forward to it with expectation and hope, remembering that God's love is not limited to this life on earth but will surround us throughout eternity. After death a person's soul permanently departs from the material plane and enters the world of the spirit, in which it can indefinitely progress and advance. The nature of that spiritual world is essentially different and superior to our earthly life here. Bahá'ís consider Heaven as nearness to God after death and Hell as distance from God or lack of awareness of spiritual realities. Our spiritual development while we are alive can be considered as preparation for our life after death.

5. What are the regular personal obligations and worship patterns of your faith community?

Each Bahá'í should

- Pray daily
- Fast during the Bahá'í fasting period
- Teach the faith to other people
- Engage in a trade or profession
- Educate his or her children
- Obey his or her government

- Make a pilgrimage to the Bahá'í holy places in Haifa, Israel, if possible
- Donate to The Bahá'í Fund
- Attend Nineteen Day Feasts, the regular worship services

The Bahá'í Faith is an entire way of life, not merely something one practices on a certain day of the week or in a particular place. Being a Bahá'í means trying to follow Bahá'u'lláh's teachings every minute of one's life. A Bahá'í strives to base his or her daily life on spiritual principles. These principles encourage development of strong unified families and communities. Work is elevated to the status of worship. Through our work we can contribute to an ever-advancing civilization.

Some worship patterns are mentioned in the personal obligations listed above. Because there is no clergy, at the Nineteen Day Feasts, which provide a time for community worship, the reading from the Holy Writing, prayer, consultation and fellowship are under the direction of members of the community.

6. What are your religion's views about revelation and the source(s) of religious authority?

All Bahá'í doctrines are primarily rooted in the revelations of Bahá'u'lláh and the supplementary interpretations of 'Abdu'l-Bahá and Shoghi Effendi. All of these are regarded as divinely authoritative. Bahá'ís believe that revelation is progressive. The successive Divine Messengers of God have accordingly revealed an ever greater measure of divine guidance appropriate to the evolutionary stages of human development. Nations are now close to the creation of a single world society—the social stage for which Bahá'u'lláh's teachings are specifically geared. Bahá'ís recognize as divine messengers Abraham, the Báb, Bahá'u'lláh, Buddha, Jesus, Krishna, Mohammad, Moses, and Zoroaster.

7. What is your faith's view about salvation?

Bahá'ís believe the only salvation in any age is to turn toward God, to accept His Messenger for that day and to follow His teachings.

"Man must be a lover of the light, no matter from what dayspring it may appear. He must be a lover of the rose, no matter in what soil it may be growing. He must be a seeker of the truth, no matter from what source it comes.

Attachment to the lantern is not loving the light."

—'Abdu'l-Bahá

BIBLIOGRAPHY FOR THE STUDY OF THE BAHÁ'Í FAITH

Esslemont, J.E. (1985) *Bahá'u'lláh and the New Era: An Introduction to the Bahá'í Faith.* Bahá'í Publishing Trust, Wilmette, Ill. An introduction to the Bahá'í Faith, originally written in 1923, updated and revised.

Hatcher, W.S. and Martin, J.D. (1984) *The Bahá'í Faith: The Emerging Global Religion.* Harper and Row, San Francisco. A definitive introduction to the history, teaching, administrative structure and community life of the Bahá'í Faith.

Hofman, D. (1992) *Bahá'u'lláh, Prince of Peace: A Portrait.* George Ronald, Oxford, UK. A portrait of the life and teachings of Bahá'u'lláh, founder of the Bahá'í Faith, on the 100th anniversary of His passing.

Johnson, L. (1987) *The Eternal Covenant.* National Spiritual Assembly of the Bahá'ís of South Africa, Johannesburg. This book focuses attention on the Covenant between God and Man as viewed by the Bahá'í Faith.

Momen, M. (editor) (1989) *A Basic Bahá'í Dictionary.* George Ronald, Oxford, UK.

National Spiritual Assembly of the Bahá'ís of the United States (1991) *The Vision of Race Unity: America's Most Challenging Issue.* Bahá'í Publishing Trust, Wilmette, Ill. The Bahá'í view of American racial problems.

Popov, Linda K. *The Virtues Guide.* Personal Power Press Int. Inc., Bowen Island, BC, Canada. Ideas for teaching moral values.

Smith, P. (1987) *The Báb and Bahá'í Religions: From Messianic Shi'ism to a World Religion.* Cambridge University Press, New York. Describes the rise of the Bahá'í Faith as a vivid example of religious change in the modern world.

Taafaki, I. (1986) *Thoughts, Education for Peace and One World: A Studybook for Moral Education.* George Ronald, Oxford, UK. A studybook on moral education with quotations from the Sacred Writings of Hinduism, Zoroastrianism, Buddhism, Judaism, Christianity, Islam, and the Bahá'í Faith.

Universal House of Justice (1985) *The Promise of World Peace.* Bahá'í Publishing Trust, Wilmette, Ill. A statement addressed "To the Peoples of the World" on the Bahá'í vision of the present conditions facing humanity and the opportunities for world peace.

Universal House of Justice, Office of Public Information (1991) *Bahá'u'lláh.* Bahá'í Publishing Trust, Wilmette, Ill. A brief presentation of the life and teachings of Bahá'u'lláh, prepared to commemorate the 100th anniversary of His passing.

ADDITIONAL BIBLIOGRAPHY OF RELATED INTEREST

Kay, C.M. (1986) *A Story of Stories.* Volturna Press, Hythe, Kent, UK. Survey of religious traditions and ideas about God, including: Hindu, Sikh, Zoroastrian, Buddhist, Confucian, Taoist, American Indian, Jewish, Christian, Islamic, Bahá'í, African.

Brown, Alan (editor) (1987) *The Shap Handbook on World Religions in Education.* Commission for Racial Equality, London. A survey of educational resources for teachers, primary and secondary classroom materials on religions and philosophies, including: Ancient Religions, Bahá'ísm, Buddhism, Christianity, Hinduism, Humanism, Islam, Jainism, Judaism, Mysticism and Meditation, Primal ("Tribal") Religions, and Sikhism.

Encyclopaedia Britannica, Inc. (1989) *Children's Britannica, v. 2,* Chicago.

Encyclopaedia Britannica, Inc. (1986) *The Encyclopaedia Britannica,* Chicago.

Buddhism

Prepared by

Buddhist Temple of San Diego
2929 Market Street
San Diego, CA 92102
619-239-0896

"Giving, discipline, patience, endeavor,
meditation and wisdom ...
Becoming a Buddha, I shall realize this vow
And give peace and tranquility to all
who are full of fear."

Sanbutsu Ge

The Buddha, example of enlightened teaching (sculpture).

INTRODUCTION AND BASIC TENETS

Buddhism is one of the world's oldest religions, and yet it is very new. People around the world are continually discovering Buddhism for the first time, and its essential truths hold much hope to those trying to cope with the challenges of modern life.

Buddhists are not preoccupied with arguments about the origins of life. Buddhism is concerned with the here-and-now, and its adherents are focused on becoming a Buddha and attaining Enlightenment, the highest wisdom. To reach this goal, one can follow the Buddha Dharma (the teachings of the Buddha) as set forth by the founder of Buddhism, Gautama. These teachings are found in the Tripitaka, ancient books in which the Teachings are preserved.

As with the other major religions, Buddhism is practiced throughout the world and has many schools, each with its emphasis on which of the Dharma teachings are most important, or which is the best pathway to Enlightenment. Shin, Zen, Nichiren, and Tibetan Buddhism are among the sects most familiar and accessible to young westerners today.

In our introduction to Buddhism, we will look briefly at its founder, its history, and its current practice as exemplified in Shin Buddhism (called Jodo Shinshu here and in Japan). Although rituals and methods of practice may differ from country to country and sect to sect, all Buddhists adhere to the same basic tenets of the Dharma and, like the historical Buddha, seek Enlightenment through wisdom and compassion.

The Founder of Buddhism

Prince Siddhartha Gautama was born over twenty-five hundred years ago in Lumbini Garden at Kapilavastu, near present-day Nepal. And yet the essential conditions of life then were no different from what they are today. Siddhartha's parents were King Suddhodana and Queen Maya, the rulers of the Sakya clan. Like many of us, Siddhartha was blessed with great material comfort. In fact, Siddhartha, as prince of a small kingdom, could have lived a life of untroubled luxury. In a legendary account of Siddhartha's awakening to the realities of life, the story of the "Four Gates" is told. One day, Siddhartha managed to stop outside one of the four gates enclosing the palace and saw a man who was old and frail. On succeeding days, Siddhartha was to go through two other gates and see the effects of sickness and death. He had been sheltered all of his life and had never seen any of these sources of suffering. Finally, when he stopped outside the fourth gate and met a religious man, the prince recognized that his existence was spiritually empty. He wanted more than to be distracted from the problems of suffering and death. He wanted to find an answer. At the age of 29, Siddhartha renounced his kingdom to devote himself entirely to a search for the truth. It must have been a painful decision, because he also had to leave his wife and his family. Many of the spiritual traditions of the time demanded utter renunciation of the world, and they often required the most severe of ascetic practices. So great was Siddhartha's desire to find the truth that he accepted these sacrifices. Year after year, he sought out spiritual teachers and underwent severe hardships.

Finally, six years after he began, and finding the life of asceticism unproductive, Siddhartha meditated on the nature of things and realized that the way to enlightenment was to examine patiently and systematically all aspects of life, including the cause and solution of suffering. He sat and meditated under a Bodhi tree and gained a deep spiritual insight into the nature of existence. He realized that it was possible to escape the chain of birth and death. He became the Buddha, the Fully Enlightened One, the Awakened One. For the next forty-five years, until his death at the age of eighty, Sakyamuni Buddha spread his teachings of wisdom and compassion.

The Teachings

The teachings of Buddhism are called the Buddha Dharma. The truth of the Buddha Dharma carries a welcome message: that wisdom and compassion can transcend the suffering caused by greed and ignorance. The Buddha Dharma further tells us that through the development of inner peace and calm, and through compassionate concern for our fellow beings, we may all attain enlightenment. These are positive messages, and the freshness and accessibility of what Buddhism teaches help account for its current appeal.

The Buddha's spiritual insight is not as mystical and abstract as it may sound at first. His great awakening was based on the realization of four concrete truths about life—the Four Noble Truths of Buddhism. The first is that life, because of its fleeting nature, is painful. The second is that this pain is caused by our desires and our attachment to worldly phenomena. The third truth is that it is possible to eliminate the suffering of existence. The fourth truth is that there is a path that leads to the elimination of suffering: the Eightfold Noble Path. The path is composed of Right Views, Right Thought, Right Speech, Right Conduct, Right Livelihood, Right Effort, Right Mindfulness, and Right Meditation. The Buddha Dharma thus asks one to know and regard life as it is, to accept life's ebb and flow, and to live one's life naturally, spontaneously, and freely.

The Path of Shin Buddhism

The Shin sect of Buddhism (or Jodo Shinshu in Japanese) is part of the Mahayana Buddhist tradition. Jodo Shinshu translates as The True Pure Land teachings. It focuses on the Vow of Amida Buddha to enlighten all beings, regardless of their backgrounds or past actions. This is a vow of sweeping power, one that promises hope and life's fulfillment to all.

Although Shinran Shonin (1173-1262) is often called the founder of Jodo Shinshu, Shinran never claimed that he was founding a new religion. Rather, Shinran merely emphasized concepts that had always existed in Buddhism. Shinran taught that the purpose of Gautama Buddha's advent on earth was to awaken people to the wisdom and compassion of Amida Buddha. Amida Buddha embodies the aspects of Infinite Wisdom, Infinite Compassion, Immeasurable Life, and Immeasurable Light, or, in other words, Enlightenment itself.

Shinran formulated the teachings after two decades of study in the Buddhist monasteries of Mt. Hiei. He came to the realization that if a person has to rely on self-generated effort, then enlightenment is impossible. He reasoned that human life is finite, human

knowledge is incomplete, and human capacity for perfect goodness is limited. Shinran renounced the monastery and left Mt. Hiei.
Shortly thereafter he met Honen, a kindly priest who taught a simple faith in Amida Buddha and the recitation of the *Nembutsu* as
an expression of faith. Shinran embraced the teachings of Honen
and built upon them. "True-Mind" or shinjin is an important ele-
ment in Shin Buddhism. The Nembutsu, "Namu Amida Butsu," or
saying the Name, is the core of Amida's vow, for Amida Buddha
communicates with us through His name. As we recite the Nembutsu, Amida's voice calls to us, and at the same time we respond
to His call. When we hear Amida's voice in our innermost being,
"True-Mind" is awakened, and we complete the oneness with
Amida; this is the true cause of our Enlightenment. The Name is
able to achieve "oneness" between Amida and the ordinary person
because the "True-Mind" is actually the Mind of Amida Buddha.
What this means is that ordinary people are able to see the world
and themselves through Amida Buddha's eyes. Only through this
enlightened view can we truly see how deeply entrenched we are
in our own karmic "evil." Only through this enlightened view can
we truly see how the way of the Nembutsu is our only hope for
enlightenment. Thus, only through this enlightened view can we
come to rely fully on the Vow of Amida Buddha, for now we truly
understand the reason for such a Vow.

The Main Temple Hall

In most Jodo Shinshu sects, the main temple hall is called the
Hondo. It is here that followers of the Nembutsu gather to listen to
the teachings and to share their lives with others. Certainly the
most striking feature of most Hondos is the beautiful and ornate
shrine. Much of the main shrine is made of wood. At the center, in
many cases, is a shrine with a gold-leafed statue of Amida Buddha
inside. Amida is depicted in the active position of standing. His
right hand is held up in a gesture of peace, his left hand is held out,
palm up, in a gesture of bestowing blessings on all beings. The
statue also leans forward, symbolizing the eternal activity of wisdom and compassion moving toward all sentient beings. Amida

Buddha, and not the statue, is the true object of veneration. Flowers are offered to symbolize the beauty and the impermanence of life. The incense purifies the air and creates the proper atmosphere for reflection. Candles symbolize the infinite light of the Buddha's Dharma teachings.

The Sangha

The Sangha, or Buddhist community, is the lifeblood of the temple. It reflects the heritage of many different backgrounds. The truth of Amida Buddha unites the Buddhist Sanghas throughout the world.

QUESTIONS AND ANSWERS

Many of the answers to these questions are from the Jodo Shin-shu Buddhism viewpoint.

1. What defines affiliation with your religious tradition?

Buddhism is based on the Four Noble Truths:

1. life, because of its fleeting nature, is painful;
2. pain is caused by our desires and our attachment to worldly phenomena;
3. it is possible to eliminate the suffering or dukha of existence;
4. the Eightfold Noble Path will lead to the elimination of suffering.

The Eightfold Noble Path consists of:

1. **Right View**—always search for the truth and the real causes of difficulties
2. **Right Thought**—always have pure thoughts
3. **Right Speech**—always speak kindly and truthfully

4. **Right Conduct**—always follow the 5 precepts of good behavior: never harm sentient life; never steal; never lie or
   deceive; never use intoxicants; live a pure and restrained life
5. **Right Livelihood**—do work that brings no harm or danger
   to others
6. **Right Effort**—always have a strong will to live a virtuous
   life
7. **Right Mindfulness**—always have a pure and thoughtful
   mind
8. **Right Meditation**—concentrate the mind on the Buddha
   and his teachings

2. What are the major holidays of your faith tradition and what does each represent?

1. **New Year's Day Service** (*Shusho E* in Japanese) Although
   it should be expressed throughout the year, on January 1,
   New Year's morning in Japan, special wishes for world peace,
   prosperity, and good heath are made, and the Four Gratitudes
   are observed.
      These Four Gratitudes include:
            gratitude to the Buddha
            gratitude to all living things
            gratitude to our parents
            gratitude to country
2. *Ho-on-ko.* Observed only by True Pure Land Buddhists on
   January 16 to commemorate the death of Shinran Shonin,
   the founder of their sect of Buddhism.
3. *Nirvana* **Day** (February 15 for Japanese; *Wesak,* celebrated
   on the first full moon day of the fifth month by Theravada
   Buddhists). The day on which Sakyamuni Buddha died. The
   actual meaning of the Sanskrit word Nirvana is "a blowing
   out as of a flame" or extinction of worldly illusions and
   passions.
4. **Spring and Autumn** *Higan.* Observed only by True Pure
   Land Buddhists and, since 1043, during the vernal and
   autumnal equinoxes. Higan is derived from the Sanskrit

word *Paramitas,* which expresses the idea that the Buddha guides people from this worldly shore to the other shore, or Nirvana.

5. **Buddha Day** (Flower Festival or *Hanamatsuri* in Japanese on April 8; celebrated on the full moon day of the fifth month in the Theravada tradition). The birth date of Siddhartha Gautama who, upon Enlightenment, became known as Sakyamuni Buddha.

6. **Shinran Shonin Day** (*Gotan E* or *Fujimatsuri* in Japanese). May 21 is the birthdate of Shinran Shonin, the founder of True Pure Land (Jodo Shinshu) Buddhism.

7. *Obon.* Observed in Japan in temples throughout the summer and on July 15 in China. Derived from Sanskrit and Chinese words, meaning salvation from suffering *(dukha)* caused by inverted views. It is an occasion for rejoicing in the enlightenment offered by the Buddha.

8. *Bodhi* **Day** (in Japan on December 8: celebrated on the first full moon day of the fifth month in the Theravada tradition). The day on which Siddhartha became enlightened while sitting in meditation under the Pippala or Bodhi tree.

9. **Year End Service** (*Joya E* in Japanese) December 31. In bringing the year to a close, events of the past year are reflected upon and gratitude is expressed to Amida Buddha, all beings, nation, and parents.

3. What are the rituals surrounding the rites of passage? Birth, Education, Marriage/Divorce, Death/Mourning.

The following are rituals within the Jodo Shinshu sect of Buddhism:

1. **Birth:** *Shosanshiki* or *Hatsu Mairi* (First visit-ceremony). The child is formally presented to the Buddha and the Sangha.

2. **Education:** Attendance at Buddhist services, Dharma or Sunday School for children, and seminars, etc. are encouraged. For ministers, a college degree in addition to postgraduate courses leading to ordination is required.

3. **Marriage:** *Kekkonshiki* (binding-marriage-ceremony). The ceremony includes chanting, the reading of the vows, and the burning of incense before the Buddha. *Sansankudo* or exchanging of nuptial cups is sometimes also performed.
4. **Divorce:** Although not encouraged, divorce is thought to be the concern only of the individuals involved.
5. **Confirmation:** *Kikyoshiki* (return-revere-ceremony). It is a simple ceremony for the layman in which the head is symbolically shaved, recalling the act of Siddhartha when he resolved to enter the spiritual path of life. A Buddhist name or *Homyo* is then given to the person who has been confirmed. Ministers receive, in addition, a *Tokudo,* or ordination bestowed by the Chief Abbot upon completion of studies.
6. **Death/Mourning:** The *Makuragyo* (pillow service), a short service held immediately following a death, includes chanting and the burning of incense before the Buddha. The *Soshiki* (burial-ceremony), usually held a few days after the death, also includes chanting, the burning of incense and remembrances by various people, and the ringing of the *Kansho,* or bell. Cremation or burial usually follows. Memorial services are held on the following anniversaries of a death: 7th, 49th and 100th days and the 1st, 3rd, 7th, 13th, 17th, 25th, 33rd, 50th, and 100th years and thereafter every 50 years.

4. Is there a view of afterlife?

The goal of all Buddhists is to become a Buddha. Generally, a person's Karma determines one's afterlife. Karma acts as the law of cause and effect. In general Buddhism, adherence to the Eightfold Noble Path assures one of Buddhahood. The *Dhammapada* states, "All that we are is the result of what we have thought; it is found on our thoughts and made up of our thoughts. If a man speaks of acts with a good thought, happiness follows him like a shadow that never leaves home." If the Eightfold Noble Path is not followed, one must repeat the cycle of rebirths.

There are many paths to Buddhahood. Jodo Shinshu Buddhists acknowledge the selfish nature of humans that makes it so difficult to follow the Eightfold Noble Path. Therefore, they rely on the wisdom and compassion of Amida Buddha's Vow to attain Nirvana, or Enlightenment.

5. What are the religious obligations/worship practices on a daily or regular basis?

Unlike temples in Japan, Jodo Shinshu temples in the United States hold weekly services, usually on Sundays, which last about one hour and consist of the ringing of the Kansho, chanting sutras, singing gathas, meditation, and messages from the minister. Most temples also offer classes for children as well as adults to learn about the Dharma. In addition, a personal or family shrine with flowers and candles is used at home for daily chanting, burning of incense, and expressing gratitude to the Buddha. One of the most important practices is gassho, or putting the hands together, with palms facing each other, holding a *nenju,* and placing it in front of the chest and the head. This represents the individual and Amida Buddha coming together and becoming one. It is done before the shrine whenever expressing gratitude. The words "Namu Amida Butsu" (the Nembutsu) are said when expressing gratitude.

6. What is the source of your religious authority?

Sakyamuni Buddha is the founder of Buddhism. His ideas, organized into the Four Noble Truths and the Eightfold Noble Path, were a radical viewpoint at the time, but over the years have become embraced by many people. The Tripitaka or "Three Baskets" are a collection of sacred books which preserve the Teachings or Dharma of the Buddha. The Pitaka consists of three parts: Sutra Pitaka, discourses of the Buddha regarding the methods of salvation; Vinaya Pitaka, moral standards; Adbidharma Pitaka, metaphysics and the philosophy of Buddhism.

In Pure Land Buddhism (Jodo Shinshu), Shinran Shonin, the founder, focuses on three sutras from the Tripitaka:

- The Larger Sutra on the Eternal Life in which Sakyamuni tells about Amida Buddha.
- The Meditation Sutra on the Eternal Buddha which tells of an actual case of a woman finding salvation through Amida Buddha.
- The Smaller Sutra on Amida Buddha in which the beauty of the Pure Land and the virtues of Amida Buddha are extolled.

7. What are your religion's view of attainment?

In general Buddhism, the goal of attaining Buddhahood, or Nirvana, is reached by following the Eightfold Noble Path. Nirvana is not a geographical or physical location, but the state of highest consciousness. Literally translated, Nirvana means the extinction of desire, or the selfish grasping state of mind and heart which makes one desire this illusory world. When one succeeds in Buddhahood, one attains the peace of Nirvana.

In Jodo Shinshu Buddhism, the Primal Vow of Amida Buddha promises Universal Enlightenment for all beings.

GLOSSARY OF TERMS

Amida. The cosmic, non-historical Buddha of infinite wisdom and compassion who lived many aeons ago; manifestation of Ultimate Truth and Sakyamuni Buddha.

Anatman. Since Buddhists do not believe in a Judeo-Christian soul, Anatman is a non-permanent substance, the non-attached, non-self, egoless "Universal Flame" that transmigrates after the physical body no long exists.

Attachment. The principle of hindrance and difficulty in seeking Enlightenment, e.g., "I," "ego," "self."

Buddha. The Enlightened One, the Supremely Awakened One; one who has become selfless, egoless, and non-attached.

Buddhahood. Becoming a Buddha; the goal of all Buddhists.

Buddhism. Belief in the release from the cycle of birth and death in the world of suffering into Enlightenment.

Dhammapada. Passages from sermons by Sakyamuni Buddha.

Dharma. The Teachings of the Buddha.

Dukha. Pain and suffering experienced by sentient beings.

Eightfold Noble Path. In general Buddhism, the path to Enlightenment: Right View, Thought, Speech, Conduct, Livelihood, Effort, Mindfulness, and Meditation.

Enlightenment. True Peace, state of non-attachment, extinction from desires, Nirvana, Pure Land; the release from the cycle of birth and death and suffering (dukha).

Four Noble Truths. The realization by Sakyamuni Buddha that life is painful because of impermanence, that the pain is a result of one's attachment to desires and worldly things, that it is possible to end this suffering, and that the way to do this is by following the Eightfold Noble Path.

Gassho. The putting together of hands with palms and fingers facing each other, holding a nenju and placing it in front of the chest, and bowing the head, symbolizing oneness with Amida Buddha; an expression of gratitude in Japanese.

Gatha. Buddhist hymnals.

Gautama. The family name of Siddhartha, the historical Buddha.

Homyo. Buddhist name.

Hondo. Main temple hall where followers gather before the shrine.

Jodo Shinshu. A major sect of Buddhism in which the selfish nature of humans is acknowledged, and the wisdom and compassion of Amida Buddha is relied upon to attain Enlightenment.

Kansho. Bell to summon followers.

Karma. Action or law of cause and effect that governs all things.

Naijin. "Inner-area" in Japanese, indicating the shrine area of the temple Hondo.

Nenju. String of beads that originally represented the 108 passions and which now in Japan symbolizes the Three Treasures.

Nichiren. A sect of Buddhism founded by Nichiren which focuses on the Lotus Sutra.

Nirvana. (see **Enlightenment**).

Primal Vow. There are 48 vows that Amida Buddha made before attaining Buddhahood. Of the 48, Jodo Shinshu calls the 18th the Primal Vow. This vow assures rebirth in the Pure Land to all who have faith in Amida Buddha.

Sakya. Name of Siddhartha's clan.

Sakyamuni. Sage of the Sakyas; the name of Siddhartha after he became Enlightened.

Sangha. Buddhist community; followers.

Shrine. The most sacred part of a Buddhist temple, where the figure of the Buddha is placed.

Siddhartha. Given name of Sakyamuni Buddha before Enlightenment.

Sutra. Buddha Dharma from sermons and discourses.

Three Treasures (Three Jewels). Buddha, Dharma, and Sangha.

Tokudo. The ordination of a Jodo Shinshu Buddhist minister bestowed by the Chief Abbot upon completion of postgraduate studies.

Tripitaka. Sacred books in which are preserved the Teachings of the Buddha from sermons and discourses.

Zen. A sect of Buddhism which focuses on meditation and self-reflection.

REFERENCES

Buddhist Temple of San Diego. *Buddhist Temple of San Diego Pamphlet.* Buddhist Temple of San Diego.

Dharma School Department. *Dharma School Service Book.* Buddhist Churches of America.

Kodani, Reverend Masao, and Hamada, Reverend Russell. *Traditions of Jodoshinshi Hongwanji-ha,* Senshin Buddhist Temple.

Shibata, Reverend George. *The Buddhist Holidays.* Buddhist Churches of America.

Sunday School Department, Buddhist Churches of America. *Lord Buddha Speaks to Me.* Buddhist Churches of America.

Tsuji, Reverend Kenryu. *Brief Introduction to Buddhism.* Bureau of Buddhist Education.

Tsuji, Reverend Kenryu. *Brief Introduction to Jodo Shin Shu.* Bureau of Buddhist Education.

Yamaoka, Bishop Seigen. *True Pure Land Buddhism: JODO SHINSHU—An Introduction.*

SUGGESTED READING

Bloom, Alfred. *Tannisho: Resource for Modern Living.* Buddhist Study Center, 1981.

Bukkyo Dendo Kyokai. *The Teaching of Buddha.* 1982. Available in Japanese-English or English-only editions.

Burtt, E.A., editor. *The Teachings of the Compassionate Buddha.* New American Library.

DeBary, Wm. T., editor. *The Buddhist Tradition in India, China and Japan.* Random House.

Kikumura, Norihiko. *Shinran: His Life and Thought.* Nembutsu Press.

Layman, Emma. *Buddhism in America.* Nelson-Hall Press.

Morgan, Kenneth, editor. *The Path of the Buddha.* Ronald Press.

Speyer, J.S. *The Jatakamala.* Motilal Barnasidas.

Suzuki, D.T. *Shin Buddhism.* Harper and Row.

The above books may be obtained from:

The Buddhist Book Store
Buddhist Churches of America
National Headquarters
1710 Octavia St.
San Francisco, California, 94109

Christianity

Prepared by

The Roman Catholic Diocese
P.O. Box 85728
San Diego, CA 92186-5728
619-490-8200

and

Ecumenical Council of San Diego County
P.O. Box 3628
San Diego, CA 92163
619-296-4557

"Yes, God so loved the world that he gave his only Son, that whoever believes in him may not die but may have eternal life."

(John 3:16)

Resurrection and Cross. "You have set us free."

INTRODUCTION AND BASIC TENETS

Christianity finds its origin in the Middle East. Biblical tradition tells us that when God created the world, the first man and woman were placed in the Garden of Paradise, where their every need was tended to. Perfect happiness was given to the first parents of the human family, Adam and Eve, and all they had to do was to honor and obey the Creator. However, evil entered the world and tempted the first man and woman to desire to be like God in all things. They disobeyed God's will and sinned against God, causing the perfect harmony of nature to be upset. In order to right the wrong, God promised a savior who, by an act of supreme obedience, would atone for the sin of disobedience of the first parents. This savior was what the Jewish people longed for and looked for through the centuries, beginning with God's revelation to Abraham. Eventually, that savior came to the world in the person of Jesus of Nazareth, who was conceived by the Holy Spirit and was born of the Virgin Mary. Jesus was born in Bethlehem and raised in Nazareth, and he preached in all of what was then known as Palestine. Ultimately, the preaching of Jesus clashed with some of the religious authorities of his day. They accused Jesus of blasphemy, which to them was a capital offense. Consequently, he was tried and executed by crucifixion under the Roman Procurator, Pontius Pilate. After Jesus' death on the cross he was placed in a tomb; three days later he rose from the dead. The resurrection of Jesus Christ from the dead proved his divinity and broke the bonds of sin and death for all people of all times. It won for humanity the salvation promised by the Creator after the fall of Adam and Eve.

During Jesus' life he gathered around himself twelve apostles who, after the death and resurrection of Jesus, went through the known world preaching the good news (Gospel) of salvation to all who would listen. This good news was at first intended only for the Jewish people, and the message was understood by the earliest followers of Jesus to be a movement within Judaism. After a very short time, however, the Gospel was preached to Jews and Gentiles alike, regardless of origin. It was at Antioch that the followers of Jesus were first called Christians (followers of Christ).

Christianity endured tremendous persecution in the first three centuries of the common era. The Roman Emperor Constantine legalized Christianity in 325 A.D./C.E., and from that point on, Christianity became the major influence of the Western world. Ultimately two centers of church authority became dominant, Rome and Constantinople. In the eleventh century, however, political and religious differences between these two centers caused a major schism in the Christian religion.

By the sixteenth century the Roman Church in the West had become a major political as well as religious force in Europe. In doing so, many people felt it had lost the zeal and enthusiasm of the early Church and earnestly sought to reform it. Martin Luther, Philip Melancthon, John Calvin, John Knox and others protested the abuses they saw in the Church and undertook what they thought to be the reform of Christianity in continental Europe. Meanwhile, Henry VIII and Elizabeth I of England made a definitive break from the authority of the Pope in their land, thus establishing a uniquely Anglican church which combined elements of both Catholicism and the new-termed Protestantism. To answer the concerns of the Protestant Reformers, the Roman Catholic Church launched the Council of Trent (1545-1563). As a result of the Council of Trent the Roman Catholic Church, for the first time in history, established universal and uniform laws governing Church practice and discipline, and clearly delineated the lines between Roman Catholic and Protestant teaching.

Protestantism continued to develop in Western Christianity over the years, with reform following reform, reformers reforming reformers. What was once a united Christianity was now unimaginably splintered: Roman Catholic, Orthodox, Anglican and Reform Protestant Christianity all competed in the proclamation of the Christian message, each claiming to have the truth while at the same time rejecting the teaching of the others. Consequently, there came to exist as many ways of approaching the Christian message and preaching it to the world as there were people willing to lead or be led.

During the next four centuries Christians would compete with one another in their mission to preach the gospel of Jesus Christ to the world. Not until 1913 would Protestants come together to begin discussing ways to work together in the missionary world, and not until 1948 would Protestants formally band together to establish the World Council of Churches. These years would initiate an era of ecumenical activity unparalleled in Christian history. Then, in 1962, Pope John XXIII convened the Second Vatican Council of the Roman Catholic Church, which led the Catholic Church to join the ecumenical movement in a serious way, especially with the promulgation of the Decree on Ecumenism in 1964. Since that time Catholic, Orthodox, Anglican and Protestant Christians have been working together to find ways to overcome their theological and cultural differences in order to find some way to restore Christian unity.

There are many different faiths in the Christian tradition. Growing in number and influence are Evangelical Christians, who are an increasingly important part of the Christian picture. Many Evangelical Christians are also called Fundamentalist Protestants who tend to be more conservative in the teachings of the Christian faith. For them the "fundamentals" of the faith are 1) The Bible is literally true and without error; 2) Jesus Christ is truly God; 3) The mother of Jesus, Mary, was a virgin when she gave birth; 4) Christ's death on the cross paid all debt for sin which humans might incur; 5) Miracles can be performed in the name of Jesus by true believers; 6) The human body will rise from the dead at the end of time; 7) Jesus Christ will come again a second time at the end of the world.

These seven fundamentals are not incompatible with the beliefs of other Christians. However, some Evangelical or Fundamentalist Christians refuse to accept the development of Christian teachings over the course of the centuries as found in many other Christian faiths.

The ecumenical task of the Christian Church is not easy, yet the majority of Christians are working more diligently than ever to be a credible witness to Christ in the world. Although serious differences continue to exist among Christians in both doctrine and discipline, the dialogues undertaken through the ecumenical movement have helped Christians to focus more clearly on the Gospel of Jesus Christ and to work with greater cooperation for the proclamation of that message to the world.

QUESTIONS AND ANSWERS

1. What defines affiliation with your religious tradition?

Belief in Jesus Christ, the Son of God, who became a human being, his life, death and resurrection making him our Lord and savior. Christians accept Jesus of Nazareth as the promised and long awaited Messiah (*Christos* in Greek; hence Christ). Acceptance of Jesus as the Christ, professed by the Sacrament of Baptism which makes a person a member of the Church (from the Greek *Kyriakon,* House of the Lord), defines a Christian.

2. What are the major holidays of your faith tradition and what does each represent?

The major holidays in common for Protestant, Catholic and Orthodox churches revolve around the life, death, and resurrection of Jesus Christ.

- **Advent:** Four weeks prior to Christmas. A time of preparation for the birth of Christ. It is the beginning of the Christian Church year.
- **Christmas:** The birth of Jesus Christ; celebrated on December 25.
- **Epiphany:** 14 days following Christmas; the visit of the Magi (wisemen) to the Christ Child.
- **Lent:** Begins with Ash Wednesday and is the six weeks prior to Easter. A time of preparation, often with fasting and other disciplines.
- **Holy Week:** The week before Easter beginning with Palm Sunday. Major days celebrated this week are Maundy Thursday (The Last Supper) and Good Friday (Crucifixion).
- **Easter Sunday:** The celebration of the resurrection of Jesus Christ, our Risen Lord. Easter is the pivotal event for the Christian faith.
- **Pentecost:** 50 days following Easter. The Gift of the Holy Spirit, considered the birthday of the Church.

General Protestant *General Roman Catholic*

3. What are the rituals of your tradition that surround the rites of passage?

Birth: Baptism or Naming ceremony (sometimes referred to as Christening).

Confirmation: Initiation in the teaching and membership of the Church; usually takes place in early teens.

Two Sacraments:

BAPTISM admits a person to the Christian Church and is administered by sprinkling or pouring water over the head of the person or by total immersion in water (often referred to as "believer's" baptism), while invoking the name of the Holy Trinity.

HOLY COMMUNION, which is also known as the Lord's Supper or Eucharist, where bread and wine are shared in Christian community as commanded by Jesus to "do this in remembrance of me." For some Christian communities it is merely a symbol, while in others it is symbolic of the real, mysterious presence of Christ within the community.

Roman Catholic and Orthodox Christianity teach that there are seven sacraments:

Baptism: admits a person to the Christian Church and is administered either by pouring water over the head of the person or by total immersion while invoking the name of the Holy Trinity.

Confirmation: seals the promise made at Baptism and conveys the grace of the Holy Spirit in a fuller way.

Holy Eucharist: is the central act of Christian worship, whereby the Last Supper of the Lord Jesus Christ is remembered and the life-giving service of Christ's death on the cross is represented to the Church. Consequently, Christians need not look back longingly for the grace-filled moment of Christ's death and resurrection because it is made real at every eucharistic celebration. Though Christ's death was a one-time historical event, it is renewed at every

General Protestant

Marriage: While not a sacrament, it is considered an important ordinance of the Church.

Divorce: Generally discouraged.

Death: Cremation is acceptable in many denominations.

Mourning: Memorial or funeral services are encouraged.

All believers are considered priests (priesthood of all believers), but certain persons are set aside by *ordination* and identified as clergy.

The manner in which these various rituals are carried out varies denominationally (for example, infant baptism vs. "believer's" adult baptism by sprinkling, pouring, or total immersion).

General Roman Catholic

Eucharist. The Holy Eucharist is the actual, physical presence of Christ among us, though under the form of bread and wine.

Penance or Reconciliation: allows the Christian person who has sinned and wandered from God and the Church to atone for his or her sins and reconcile with God and the Church.

Holy Matrimony: sanctifies married life between a man and a woman.

Holy Orders: confers on men the duties as deacons, presbyters (priests) and bishops for the spiritual welfare of the Church. Ordination in the Roman Catholic and Orthodox Churches is for men only because it was only the twelve apostles to whom Christ gave authority in the Church.

Anointing of the Sick with blessed oil combined with prayer is used as a means to restore physical and spiritual health to people who have fallen ill, as mandated by the Holy Scriptures (Mark 6:13; James 5:14).

General Protestant *General Roman Catholic*

4. Does your tradition have a view of an afterlife? If so, describe it briefly.

A life lived in Jesus Christ assures the believer of a continued relationship with Christ after physical death.

When Christians die, those who have placed their trust in the Lord Jesus Christ and have lived a holy, good life are reborn to eternal life with God where there is no more weeping or tears. When the faithful Christian goes to heaven we are assured by St. Paul, "Eye has not seen, ear has not heard, nor has it so much as dawned on man what God has prepared for those who love him" (1 Cor 2:9).

5. What are the regular personal obligations and worship patterns of your faith's community?

The Ten Commandments and the Teachings of Jesus are accepted as the standard for moral behavior. Sunday is the generally accepted day of worship. Support of the church is expected, and while tithing is considered the ideal, financial commitments vary greatly. Stewardship also involves tithing of time, talents, and personal gifts.

Worship has various expressions from the highly liturgical to the extremely informal. The Worship Service provides a sense of community. Individual meditation, prayer and Bible study are encouraged.

Worship of God at the Sunday Eucharist is the norm for Sabbath obligation.

General Protestant   *General Roman Catholic*

6. What are your religion's views about revelation and the source(s) of religious authority?

The Holy Bible, in its entirety, is considered the source of authority, emphasizing the teachings of Jesus and early Christianity.

Revelation: Scripture is considered inspired by God, with continued guidance provided by the Holy Spirit.

Church councils and denominational assemblies shape doctrine.

Authority in the Roman Catholic Church is found primarily in the Word of God, as revealed in both the written scriptures, the Holy Bible, and the oral teachings of the Church, Sacred Tradition, passed down to the present day from the time of the apostles. The chief religious leader is the Pope, the Bishop of Rome, who in concert with the other bishops of the Church possesses and maintains the teaching authority of the apostles themselves, and whose main task is to preserve the unity of the Church and guarantee the purity and truth of the Church's teachings (doctrines). The Pope and the bishops are the primary teachers of the faith of the Church. The Catholic Church teaches that the Pope speaks infallibly (preserved from error and guaranteed to be true) only

General Roman Catholic

when speaking on matters of
faith and morals and when
speaking as Vicar (personal
representative) of Christ and
ex cathedra, from the chair of
Peter, the chief of the apostles.
Councils of bishops held
throughout history have con-
sistently defined the doctrine
of the Christian Faith as understood and practiced by Roman
Catholics, the most recent
Council having been the
Second Vatican Council,
1962-65.

7. What is your faith's view of salvation?

Salvation comes to the world from God through the saving pas-
sion, death and resurrection of Jesus Christ. Salvation through
Christ is for all people, of all places, of all times. When the Gospel
of Jesus Christ is effectively preached by Christians, Christ will be
accepted by the hearer.

GLOSSARY OF TERMS

Church. The term signifies the body of Christian believers. Its
roots are Greek, coming from *Kyriakon* (House of the Lord), to
German (*Kirche*), to Old English (*Kirk*) to the modern term *Church*.

Christ. In Hebrew, the term for the long-awaited savior is *Messiah*.
This translates in Greek as *Christos,* from which the word *Christ* is
derived.

Ecumenism. Greek root, *Oikumene,* meaning "the whole inhab-
ited world." Ecumenism is the movement within Christianity to
restore the broken unity of the Church through inter-Christian

dialogue and cooperation. A related term would be "Ecumenical Movement."

Eucharist. The *Eucharist* is one of the Sacraments of the Church. Its root is Greek which means "thanksgiving." The Eucharist is also known as Holy Communion and the Lord's Supper, where bread and wine are shared in the Christian assembly as commanded by Jesus to "do this in memory of me" (Luke 22:19). In some Christian communities the Eucharist is merely symbolic and in others it is symbolic of the real, mysterious presence of Christ within the community. For other Christians, however, most notably Roman Catholic and Orthodox, the Eucharist is the actual sharing of the body and blood of Jesus under the form of bread and wine. When the Eucharist is thus shared, the death and resurrection of Jesus are re-presented to the Church to encourage and spiritually nourish the Church in the world.

Gospel. Greek in origin, *gospel* means "Good News." The good news of the life, death and resurrection of Jesus, and of the atonement (payment of any debt) for sin and the salvation of the world won for us in Christ is what Christians are called to preach to the world.

Heaven. *Heaven* is that state of being or condition that all who have gained salvation enjoy. Heaven is not a physical place but a spiritual reality. All who attain heaven enjoy the beatific vision, that is, total union with God for all eternity.

Lent. Old English is the origin for the world *Lent*. It derives from *lencten,* which means "springtime." In the springtime of each year there is a period of six weeks prior to Easter, the Christian celebration of the resurrection of Christ from the dead, that is a time of spiritual renewal for Christians. The six weeks are marked by greater efforts at fasting, prayers and almsgiving.

Patriarch. A *Patriarch* is the spiritual leader of one of the five original centers of the Church. A Patriarch's authority once extended over specific geographical areas and included ordaining bishops to oversee the Church in a local area. In modern times, the title Patriarch has been given to the heads of each of the autonomous Orthodox Churches of Eastern Europe. Patriarch is also a title of honor given to the presiding bishop of some of the Eastern Rites of the Roman Catholic Church.

Pope. The *Pope* is the title given to the Bishop of Rome, the Patriarch of the West, the temporal spiritual leader of the Roman Catholic Church. The term comes from the Latin root *papa* meaning "father." The term was originally used by any bishop in the West, but in 1073 Pope Gregory VII restricted its use only for the Bishop of Rome. The Pope is elected by selected bishops of the Roman Catholic Church called *Cardinals,* a term which in Latin means "hinge," whose chief function it is to select the new Pope at the death of the incumbent.

Sacraments. The *Sacraments* are sacred, visible signs of God's presence, which manifest the faith of the Church and through which God's free gifts of grace and life are offered. In Christianity, Roman Catholic and Orthodox Christians define seven sacraments: Baptism, Holy Eucharist, Confirmation, Penance, Matrimony, Holy Orders and Anointing of the Sick. Reform Protestants generally adhere to two sacraments, Baptism and Holy Eucharist (Lord's Supper or Communion).

Schism. This term has its origin in Greek and means "tear" or "rent." It is "formal and willful separation from the unity of the Church" (Oxford Dictionary of the Christian Church, p. 1242) and is generally used to describe the split between the Western and Eastern Christian churches in the eleventh century, establishing the first major division of a formerly unified Christianity.

Stewardship. This defines the responsible use of time, talent and material goods on the part of believing Christians for the building up of the Church and the welfare of its people.

Ten Commandments. In the Book of Exodus in the Bible, God gave the prophet Moses ten commandments to guide all aspects of life for God's people. Not only do the Ten Commandments establish the basic moral code for Christians, but they establish the basis of the human relationship with God.

Tithing. In the Bible, God's people are expected to provide for the support of the ministers of the Lord and the synagogue or church property. The Christian concept of tithing today is that ten percent of an individual's income should be returned to the Lord, through donations to the Church, as a sign of gratitude for what has been received and as a means to care for the temporal needs of the Church and assistance to the poor. Tithing, it should be noted, is the ideal form of Christian stewardship, but it is not always fulfilled.

Trinity. The dogma of the *Trinity* is the central dogma of Christian theology. There is but one God (monotheism) but the one God exists in three persons. In its strictest sense, the Trinity is a mystery and cannot be fully explained in human terms to satisfy human understanding. The three persons of the one God are Father (Creator), Son (Redeemer), and Holy Spirit (Sustainer). It is essential to note that the three persons of the Trinity compose one God, not three; the one God has three distinct yet equal persons, working simultaneously yet distinctly.

SUGGESTED READING

Bihlmeyer, Karl, and Hermann Touchie. *Church History.* 3 vols. Vol. 3, *Modern and Recent Times.* Westminster: Newman Press, 1955.

Callahan, Daniel, ed., *Christianity Divided: Protestant and Roman Catholic Theological Issues.* London: Sheed and Ward, 1961.

Cross, F.L., and E.A. Livingston, eds. *The Oxford Dictionary of the Christian Church,* 2nd ed. Oxford: Oxford University Press, 1974.

Dulles, Avery, S.J. *Models of the Church.* New York: Doubleday and Company, Inc., 1974.

Fouyas, Methodios, *Orthodoxy, Roman Catholicism and Anglicanism.* London, New York, Toronto: Oxford University Press, 1972.

Hillerbrand, Hans. *Christendom Divided: The Protestant Reformation.* London: Hutchinson, Corpus: New York, 1971.

Mead, Frank. *Handbook of Denominations in the United States.* Nashville: Abingdon Press, 1980.

Tillard, Jean. *The Bishop of Rome.* Tr. by John de Stage. London: SPCK, 1973.

Whalen, William. *Separated Brethren: A Survey of Protestant, Anglican, Eastern Orthodox and Other Denominations in the United States.* Huntington, IN: Our Sunday Visitor, Inc., 1979.

Hinduism

Prepared by

The Vedanta Society of Southern California
1440 Upas Street
San Diego, CA 92103
619-291-9377

"As all the rivers of the world constantly
pour their waters into the ocean, but the
ocean's grand, majestic nature remains
undisturbed, so even though all the senses
bring in sensations from nature, the
ocean-like heart of the sage knows
no disturbance, knows no fear."

Bhagavad-Gita, 2:70

*Thousands of Indian women carrying pitchers of
holy water for the beginning of a grand Hindu
religious ritual "Ashwamedh Yajna."*

BASIC TENETS

Hinduism has a longer history than any of the major religions of the world. This combined with the fact that it encourages free religious experimentation has made of Hinduism a vast and diverse religion—so vast and diverse that some scholars claim it is more like a collection of related religions than a single religion. There are, according to scholars, more similarities between Judaism, Christianity, and Islam than between some of the sects of Hinduism. But there are certain unifying elements which allow us to speak of Hinduism as a whole.

1. First of all, a Hindu is one who accepts the spiritual authority of the Vedas, the ancient scriptures of the Hindus. There are different ways, however, in which the Vedas may be accepted. Some Hindus accept them literally, as fundamentalists in all religions do with their scriptures.

Most Hindus, however, take only the portions which deal with supersensuous truths (the nature of God and souls) as the highest authority. This is not a modern innovation due to scientific education, but it is an ancient tradition. The reason given for this view is that there is no other way to learn about supersensuous truths except through revelation; any teaching in the scriptures which can also be discovered through the mind and senses is not authoritative, unless the other methods of inquiry confirm it. This attitude in part explains why there has been no conflict between Hinduism and modern science.

For a Hindu, faith in the scriptures is not an end, but the beginning. The scriptures point the way to the truth. Having a provisional "working faith," a Hindu is to follow the path indicated in the scriptures until his or her faith is confirmed through experience.

2. There is a spiritual reality, known as Brahman, which is the foundation of this universe. And Brahman is formless, infinite, all-pervading spirit, neither male nor female. The universe comes out of It, and rests in It.

Brahman enters into relationship with living beings as the personal God of love. Because Brahman is infinite, It manifests as the personal God in countless ways. That is the basis for the many Deities in India. They are different faces of the one infinite God. No one view of God can exhaust the divine nature. God is Father, Mother, Friend, Child, Beloved, Lord, and infinitely more. God can manifest with form (pictured in the many different images worshiped in India) or without form.

In fact, since Brahman is the reality underlying the universe, anything in the universe can serve as a symbol or image of God. No one in India has ever worshiped a stick or stone: they worship God who dwells within the image. The mind cannot conceive of pure spirit, so the image gives a focus for the mind, charged with symbolic power; and through that the devotee can enter into direct relationship with the Divine.

3. The soul of each living being is divine. According to some, the soul is one with God; according to others, it is a spark of God; but according to all Hindus, the soul is eternal, uncreated, all-knowing, and pure by nature. Due to ignorance it appears to lose these characteristics.

4. There are four goals of life according to the Hindu. One is enjoyment of legitimate pleasure. The second is prosperity or acquisition of the means to enjoy life. The third is dharma or righteousness. Righteousness is a goal of life because it puts us in harmony with the laws of the universe, bringing peace of mind and strength of character. The first two—pleasure and acquisition—have to be in harmony with righteousness, the third, to be legitimate. The fourth is liberation from earthly bondage through the direct experience of God and soul. We must, says the Hindu, in this or a future life regain our lost kingdom: the innate purity and divinity of the soul, fully aware of its relationship with Brahman.

5. All Hindus accept the law of karma, which applies Newton's Third Law of Motion to the moral sphere: for every action there is an equal and opposite reaction. If we do good, good is returned. If we do harm, harm is returned. Our conditions in life are set up by

our own past actions. By action with wisdom now, we can improve our future circumstances.

6. Our karmic accounts are not balanced in the course of one life, so the law of karma requires that we be born again and again in an attempt to balance our karmic debts. This is reincarnation. After death, we take birth again in whatever circumstances our past karma has earned for us.

The goal of the Hindu is not simply to settle our karmic accounts. Nor is the Hindu's goal to be born again and again in better and better circumstances. The Hindu's goal is to rise above the compulsion of karma and rebirth through the experience of Brahman, who is eternally free and blissful. Such experience frees one from the wheel of birth and death.

7. There is a moral law known as dharma which supports this universe. This law is not made by the decree of God; it is an impersonal law which is part of the structure of the universe itself, like gravity. By being in tune with dharma, one is in harmony with the universe. By contradicting dharma, one is out of harmony and degenerates. God is therefore not a judge in Hinduism. If I put my hand in fire, I don't blame God for burning me, but recognize that I have transgressed a physical law. So if I go against the moral order of the universe and am brought to harm, I shouldn't blame God but my own ignorance, says the Hindu. If some harm comes to me which is greater than any harm which I can remember having done, the Hindu says that an ancient debt from a past life is being balanced.

8. Hinduism, like Christianity, teaches that God incarnates in human form. But the Hindus believe that God has incarnated several times in the past and will incarnate in the future also, according to the needs of the time. An Incarnation of God is known to Hindus as an Avatar. Since the introduction of Christianity into India, most Hindus accept Christ as an Avatar, seeing that his life and teachings are so closely parallel to the lives and teachings of their own Avatars. But they reject the doctrine that he is the only way of salvation.

Not all Hindus believe in the Incarnation of God. In fact, not all believe in a Personal God.

9. Since the time of the Vedas the Hindus have believed that religion is one—that different "religions" are really different paths leading to the same goal: the experience of truth or communion with God. As the ancient Rig-Veda says, "Truth is one; sages call it by various names." Many religious texts of the Hindu scriptures echo this theme of harmony and acceptance. To the Hindu, tolerance is only bigotry with a friendly face. The Hindu teaches acceptance.

10. Besides the Vedas (which include the Upanishads or Vedanta), there are many other scriptures of the Hindus, some of them sectarian, others universally accepted. The Vedas are the most authoritative. Next in authority comes the Bhagavad-Gita. Other scriptures are accepted insofar as they agree with the Vedas and are not contradicted by reason or experience.

11. Caste conventions are not an intrinsic part of Hinduism. Caste is a social institution, and the nature of the system has changed a great deal over three millennia. The Smritis or Hindu law books deal with such matters, and such conventions are said to change with time and circumstance and are therefore not of eternal validity.

SPECIAL POINTS OF SENSITIVITY FOR HINDUS

1. Westerners usually direct their attention to some external observances of the Hindus which seem to them bizarre, completely missing the inner significance of what they see. Cow worship, image worship, Hindu ritual and mythology, all of these are based on deeply considered philosophical principles. But if only the external forms are looked at without understanding the meaning, it distorts the meaning.

Image worship in particular is often looked upon in the West not only as superstition but as something evil. Even to a Hindu, image worship is optional, but for their worship to be treated as an evil is offensive to any Hindu.

2. Hindus resent the inordinate attention given to the caste system whenever Westerners deal with Hinduism. It is as if that were the central defining characteristic of the religion, whereas in fact it is a social institution which in its pure form had scriptural sanction.

Modern Hindus themselves are embarrassed by the undeniable abuses of the caste system and will readily admit such abuses. But the negative way in which Westerners always deal with the caste system is offensive because it overlooks several important factors. On the negative side:

- The usual treatment of the caste system overlooks the great liberalizing forces working within Hinduism itself over the millennia. Again and again great saints arose (in India all reform has come through the religion) who embraced in their fold all communities, who taught universal compassion, who stressed that service to all beings is the highest worship, and who taught that in God's eye, there is no caste.

Even more significantly, there are positive aspects to the caste system which are usually overlooked:

- It is based on a natural, observable classification of people found in all societies: intellectuals, administrators, business people and laborers. Of course, in a religious society like India, the intellectuals are also priests. And in an ancient society, administrators are kings, ministers, and warriors. So the four classes are priests, rulers, merchants, and laborers. In time these four primary classes became hereditary. And eventually they became divided and subdivided into countless castes. In its original form as a four-fold class structure, it is found universally.

- The practical purpose of the caste system was to reduce competition and ensure security, much like trade unions. Even to this day it has given to Hindus high and low a feeling of belonging, of connectedness: everyone has one's part to contribute. Everyone is needed.
- The caste system was never developed out of the greed of the higher castes. In fact, the brahmins were among the poorest of the population. The higher the caste, the more restrictions, based on the idea that higher position entails greater responsibility and greater self-sacrifice.
- The caste system gave to India a vital stability which allowed it to live. And until foreign conquests robbed her of her famed wealth, she prospered. All other ancient civilizations have come to an end: they are studied by archaeologists and historians. But India has had an uninterrupted course of cultural life since Vedic times, in spite of suffering invasion after invasion.
- The system allowed communities with widely differing social customs, mores, taboos, and institutions to live side by side without friction. As the Vedic Aryans spread through the subcontinent encountering different communities, they didn't demand conformity to their own social ways nor did they resort to genocide, the two methods used in most other cultures to avoid the friction that comes from social diversity. Rather they allowed the different communities to continue their own cultural life. It was the caste system which allowed this.

QUESTIONS AND ANSWERS

1. What defines affiliation with your religious tradition?

For much of Hinduism's long history, it was an ethnic religion. One was usually born a Hindu. But there were times before the growth of Islam when Hindu affiliation was open to foreigners, for Hinduism spread to Afghanistan in the West and to Bali in the East; Hindu teachers lived in the Mediterranean world around the time of Christ, and today Hinduism has again spread to many countries of the world. Though most Hindus are still born such of Indian parents, a Hindu is primarily one of any race or culture who accepts the spiritual authority of the Vedas. Usually a Hindu has also gone through certain rites of passage like investiture with the sacred thread, or spiritual initiation through which one receives meditation instructions and connection to a lineage of spiritual teachers.

2. What are the major holidays of your faith tradition, and what does each represent?

There are countless holidays in the Hindu tradition, differing from place to place and sect to sect. Some of the major holidays which are widely observed are New Year's Day (usually in February or March, differing from area to area), Rama Navami or the birthday of the divine incarnation Rama (March–April), Vasanti Puja in which God as Mother is worshiped in the spring (March–April), Guru-purnima when spiritual preceptors are honored (June–July), Ratha-yatra or the chariot festival associated with the divine incarnation Krishna (June–July), Krishna Janmashtami or the birthday of Krishna (August–September), Ganesha Chaturthi when the God Ganesha is worshiped (August–September), Navaratri or the nine-day festival during which God as Mother is worshiped (September–October), Lakshmi Puja when Lakshmi or the Goddess of Fortune is worshiped (October), Kali Puja or the worship of the Goddess Kali (October–November), Deepawali or the Festival of Lights (October–November), Saraswati Puja when the Goddess of Learning is worshiped (January–February), and Shiva-ratri or the night of Shiva (February–March). The Indian calendar is a luni-solar calendar, so the dates change in relation to the Western calendar from year to year.

3. What are the rituals surrounding the rites of passage?

There are various rites of passage for Hindus—some list forty-eight, some sixteen, some nine—and they may differ somewhat from sect to sect. The rites are known as "samskaras," which may be translated either as "enculturations" or "purifications," the main purposes being: (a) the transmission of culture, (b) the purification and trans-formation of the animal man/woman into the spiritual, (c) the warding off of inauspicious influences and attraction of the bene-ficial, and finally (d) the self-expression of joy and accomplishment at various stages of life. The most important rites are the prenatal rites like the hair-parting of the pregnant mothers, birth cere-monies, name-giving, first outing, first feeding of solid food, ton-sure, learning of the alphabet, initiation with the sacred thread which allows study of the Vedas (usually by the age of twelve), mar-riage, the funeral ceremony, and offerings to deceased ancestors.

4. Is there a view of afterlife?

All sects of Hindus believe not only in an afterlife but in a "prior life": they believe in the eternality of the soul. A person's actions in this life determine the nature of their next life. Heavens and hells are temporary states of reward and punishment for extraordinary good or evil deeds. After death one might, according to one's karma, be reborn on this earth, usually in human form, though reverting to animal forms is also possible, or one might go to a temporary heaven or hell, or one might go to the realm of the ancestors where one is joined for an extended period by friends and family. One might even through extraordinary merit become a minor deity— for the minor deities are positions held by meritorious humans, long-lasting positions of great power, wisdom and blessedness, but still temporary. The goal of the Hindu, however, is not transmi-gration but spiritual freedom through the direct knowledge of God and soul.

5. What are the religious obligations/worship practices on a daily or regular basis?

Hinduism has always been a personal religion, never an organized or church-centered religion. It has been perpetuated by family and village tradition and by the tie between a teacher (guru) and his/her disciples. (There are and have been many women gurus.) A Hindu household has five debts which are to be repaid daily: a) a debt to God, which is repaid by prayer, worship, and meditation; b) a debt to the ancient sages, which is repaid by study of the scriptures; c) a debt to one's ancestors, which is repaid by living honorably and by carrying on the family line; d) a debt to other people, repaid by charity; and e) a debt to lower beings, repaid by acts of kindness like feeding. For a monk or nun who renounces personal property and marriage, there is no obligation other than the search for spiritual truth: that itself is considered the highest service to society.

For a description of this goal of spiritual freedom, see the answer to question 7, "What is your religion's view of salvation?"

6. What is the source of your religious authority?

Orthodox Hindus accept the Vedas as revealed scriptures, though there is difference of opinion concerning just what that means. (See the "Basic Tenets.") They also believe that a human being who has become established in transcendent wisdom has tapped the source of revelation: such a person's words are given great reverence. But the scriptures are the measuring rod, for they serve to show us whether a person is actually in a transcendent state or just self-deluded.

7. What is your religion's view of salvation?

Hindus don't normally use the word "salvation." They speak in terms of illumination, enlightenment, liberation, attainment. Most Hindus accept the doctrine of divine grace; most believe that without the grace of God one cannot attain illumination. But they still don't think in terms of "salvation" because Hindus believe that the soul in essence is pure and perfect already. We are not sinners by nature but pure and perfect beings who have forgotten our true nature and therefore commit all sorts of mistaken actions. Evil comes from delusion, not from our inherent nature. The grace of God reminds us of our forgotten nature and wipes away the effects of evil karma.

Consistent with the great diversity in Hinduism, there are different forms of attainment, which are not considered contradictory to one another, but dependent on temperament. Some retain a sense of personal identity, but are fully aware of the presence of

God; they dwell in perpetual adoration and service of God, possessing infinite wisdom and love and enjoying eternal beatitude. Others seek to realize their identity with Brahman, which is a timeless state of infinitude—infinite being, infinite knowledge, infinite joy. Because it is timeless, it can never come to an end nor be interrupted. After attainment, some seek to retain a sense of enlightened individuality to render help to other beings who are still bound.

GLOSSARY OF TERMS

ashram. (1) Also ashrama: a place of spiritual retreat. It can be a monastery, or it can be a lay community, or a mixture. (2) Any one of the four stages of life into which a person's life is divided: celibate student's life, householder life, life of retirement and contemplation, and life of renunciation (monastic life).

Atman. The Self or soul. It is the true spiritual Self, as opposed to the ego or assumed sense of individuality. In Christian terms, it is the image of God within.

Avatar. Literally one who "crosses over" or "crosses down," an Avatar is an incarnation of God, who has "crossed over" from the Divine to the human plane of existence. Hindus believe that there have been several Avatars in the past, and will be more in the future, according to the needs of the time. Some are known today only through legend, others are quite historical.

Bhagavad-Gita. The most loved and studied of Hindu scriptures, and also the most translated. Coming after the close of the Upanishadic age, it takes the teachings of the Upanishads and puts them in a dynamic form, related to the problems of life. Mahatma Gandhi said that whenever he faced a problem in life, he never failed to find its answer in the Gita. It takes the form of a dialog between Krishna and his disciple Arjuna on the battlefield. It is a part of the epic poem The Mahabharata, and is dated variously between the sixth and second centuries BCE.

Bharata. The official name of India, named after an ancient sage-king.

Brahman. The infinite and transcendent divine Reality, beyond space and time, beyond definition, beyond all our concepts and ideas, beyond even the idea of personality.

Deities. Aspects or "faces" of the one infinite God. Looking from the human standpoint, no one view of the Divine can be exhaustive. Looking from the standpoint of divine revelation, God manifests in different ways to different people, according to their temperament and capacity. For these two reasons there are in Hinduism many Deities, but one God.

dharma. The moral order of the universe.

Ganesha. A strange-looking but much-adored Deity, he is the elephant-headed Deity who removes all obstacles and grants success. As such, his worship comes before all important undertakings.

guru. A spiritual teacher, who may be male or female.

Kali. An aspect of the Divine Mother which is shocking when first encountered and profound when understood. Four-armed, she holds in two hands a severed head and sword, and with the other two hands she offers boons and freedom from fear. The basic idea is that both life and death are part of God's cosmic economy: both are gifts of the Divine Mother. When seen in that light we fear neither life nor death, for both are Her gifts.

karma. The doctrine that every action leaves its mark on our character and also brings a return from the cosmos: good actions bring good, bad actions bring misery. The law of retribution.

Krishna. A person of vast importance in Hinduism, he is considered an incarnation of God. His life is shrouded in legend and myth to such an extent that an historical core cannot now be determined. His worship was already firmly and widely established in India by the time of Alexander the Great's expedition. He is the teacher of the Bhagavad-Gita, and the central figure in the Mahabharata and Srimad Bhagavatam, all very important works of the post-Vedic period.

Lakshmi. The Goddess of good fortune, associated with Vishnu.

Mahabharata. The longest epic in the world. It contains the Bhagavad-Gita and other important Hindu texts. Along with the Ramayana, it has influenced India more than any other text, giving heroes and ideals and practical guidance to Hindus for at least 2,500 years.

mantra. (1) A verse of the Rig-Veda. (2) A sacred name of God, considered to have spiritual power inherent in it. Its repetition is said to bring purity of mind, concentration, and spiritual beatitude.

maya. Cosmic ignorance. Maya is not so much a theory as a statement about the human condition: the contradictions inherent in life, the contradiction between our infinite desire to know and the limitations put on our knowledge, between our desire for unlimited happiness and the very limited means of fulfillment available, between our desire to live forever and the shortness of life, between our sense that we are free agents and the continual bondage we find ourselves in. The Hindu seeks freedom from Maya.

namaste. A popular greeting among Hindus which literally means "Salutations to you." It is said in recognition of the presence of divinity within each being.

Om. Also spelled Aum, it is the most sacred and most universal symbol of Divinity in Hinduism. It is considered to be the primal Word of God, out of which all creation has come. As such, it is the most perfect name of God, and represents both the immanent, Personal God and the transcendent Brahman.

prana. The life-force, known as *chi* in Chinese thought, which distinguishes the living from the non-living.

puja. Hindu ritual worship.

Rama. One of the most popular incarnations of God, or Avatars, of Hinduism, Rama was the king of Ayodhya and hero of the great epic *Ramayana*. Like Krishna, his life is shrouded in legend, leaving no certain historical core. He seems to have lived earlier than Krishna.

Ramayana. The epic tale of Rama, an incarnation of Vishnu, which has been instrumental in fashioning attitudes toward duty, proper family relationships, the ideal of womanhood, righteous behavior, the ideal ruler, true heroism, etc. It belongs to the period just after the Vedic Age, or several centuries before Christ.

Rig-Veda. The first and oldest of the four Vedas. The others are the Sama-Veda, the Yajur-Veda, and the Atharva-Veda.

sadhu. A holy man.

samadhi. A state of unitary consciousness which leads to the knowledge of God and soul. There are different degrees of samadhi. The highest degree grants transcendent wisdom, union with God, and immortal bliss. It can be experienced in this life itself, though such a high state in life is rare.

Sanatana Dharma. Literally the "eternal religion," this is the name by which Hindus knew their religion. "Hinduism" is a foreign term used to describe the people living near the Sindhu River.

Sanskrit. The classical language which was used until modern times for religious and philosophical discourse. The Vedas are written in Vedic, an older form of Sanskrit. Other scriptures are in classical Sanskrit. It is the most ancient surviving form of the Indo-European family of languages.

Sarasvati. The Goddess of learning.

Shakti. Literally "power," Shakti refers to the Divine Mother, or God as Mother of the Universe. She is the dynamic aspect of Divinity. Though Brahman is beyond all distinction of male and female, it manifests as the Personal God who can be seen as male or female. Worship of God as Mother is very common all over India. It is believed by many that the transcendent aspect of God (Brahman) can be reached only through the grace of Shakti.

Shiva. A Deity or aspect of God worshiped all over India, often misidentified by Christian missionaries as the devil, since he is sometimes pictured carrying a trident, wearing a serpent around his neck, and dwelling in a cremation ground. Such images in Indian mythology are deeply symbolic and philosophical. Shiva means "auspicious." The serpent represents divine knowledge. Shiva dwells in the cremation ground both because he reminds people of the transience of life, and because he is the refuge of the departing soul. Sometimes he is represented as the cosmic dancer: this universe of creation, activity and destruction is his dance.

Swami. A title given to an ordained Hindu monk. Literally "master," the title refers to the ideal monk who is master of his own mind, senses, and passions. Grammatically the word Swami is masculine. Though nowadays ordained Hindu nuns are sometimes called Swamis, the more proper term is "Pravrajika," meaning "one who has gone forth from the home."

Upanishads. At the end of each of the four Vedas come several books called the Upanishads, which are the philosophical high point of Vedic thought. They are the most authoritative texts for a Hindu.

Vedanta. The end (*anta*) of the Vedas, or the Upanishads. Vedanta also means by association the religious and philosophical tradition which has grown out of the Upanishads. Practically all Hindus of all denominations today are followers of Vedanta.

Vedas. The ancient scriptures of the Hindus, and the most ancient scriptures of the world. Scholars date the period of their creation conservatively at 1500-500 B.C.E. Some modern scholars put the date as far back as 6000-5000 B.C.E.

Vishnu. A Deity or "face" of God who is especially associated with ideas of beauty, sublimity, protection. Direct worship of Vishnu has been lessened by the fact that the incarnations of God—Krishna, Rama, Chaitanya and others—are all said to be his incarnations. They are worshiped much more than Vishnu himself. Most Hindus are worshipers of Shiva or of Shakti or of Vishnu and his incarnations.

yoga. Meaning "union," yoga comes from the same Indo-European root as the English word "yoke." It refers to the state of union between the Atman or soul and God. It more commonly refers to a path leading to such union. There are many forms of yoga in the sense of spiritual path: the yoga of devotion, the yoga of knowledge, the yoga of selfless work and the yoga of meditation. What Americans usually think of as yoga is hatha yoga, a minor school of physical and mental culture aimed at gaining control of the body and mind.

SUGGESTED READING

Huston Smith, *World's Religions.*

The Upanishads, translated by Swami Prabhavananda and Frederick Manchester.

Bhagavad-Gita: The Song of God, translated by Swami Prabhavananda and Christopher Isherwood.

The Essential Teachings of Hinduism: Daily Readings from the Sacred Texts, edited by Kerry Brown.

Swami Prabhavananda, *The Spiritual Heritage of India.*

What Religion Is: In the Words of Swami Vivekananda, edited by Swami Vidyatmananda.

Living Wisdom, edited by Pravrajika Vrajaprana.

Swami Prabhavananda, *The Sermon on the Mount According to Vedanta.*

Swami Atmarupananda, *Vedanta: A Religion, A Philosophy, A Way of Life.*

Islam

Prepared by:

The Council of Islamic Education
P.O. Box 20186
Fountain Valley, CA 92728-0186

and

American Islamic Services Foundation
7710 Balboa Avenue, Suite 219B
San Diego, CA 92111
(619) 279-1979 or (619) 697-8808

"In the name of Allah, most gracious,
most merciful."

Muslims pray in the upper gallery of the main mosque in the old walled city on the occasion of Eid al-Fitr, which celebrates the end of the holy fasting month of Ramadan.

INTRODUCTION

The American Islamic Services Foundation (AISF), a member of the Interreligious Council of San Diego, appointed the Council on Islamic Education (CIE) to represent Muslims on all education issues on the Interreligious Council. AISF has commissioned CIE to participate in preparing documents and attending meetings on its behalf. This document was prepared by Shabbir Mansuri, Director of CIE, with the help of Muslim scholars and educators (Dr. Muzammil Siddiqi, California State University of Fullerton and Director of the Islamic Center of Orange County, Dr. Abdussattar U. Shaikh, Vice President, Languages and International Projects, American Commonwealth University, Imam Sharif Battikhi of AISF and Semeen Issa of the Los Angeles Unified School District).

The following section on Islam touches upon a broad range of topics within a limited amount of space. Moreover, the content of this section conforms closely to the California History-Social Science Framework's criteria for teaching about Islam in public school instructional materials. Prevalent ground rules for teaching about religion in general, which relate to issues such as sensitivity and balance, among others, have also been taken into consideration in the preparation of this material.

BASIC TENETS

Introductory Information

Islam and Muslims

The Arabic term *Islam* has several interrelated meanings, including "surrender," "submission," "commitment" and "peace." Commonly, *Islam* refers to the monotheistic religion revealed to Muhammad ibn (son of) Abdullah between 610 and 632 of the common era (C.E.). The name *Islam* was instituted by the *Qur'an,* the sacred scripture revealed to Muhammad. For believers, Islam is not a new religion—rather, it represents the last reiteration of the primordial message of God's Oneness, a theme found in earlier monotheistic religious traditions.

Though Islam can be described as a religion, it is viewed by its adherents in much broader terms. Beyond belief in specific doctrines and performance of important ritual acts, Islam is practiced as a complete and natural way of life, designed to bring God into the center of one's consciousness, and thus one's life.

The word *Muslim* means "*one who submits (to God)*." Islam teaches that everything in Creation—microbes, plants, animals, mountains and rivers, planets, and so forth—is "muslim," testifying to the majesty of the Creator and submitting to His divine laws. Human beings, also, are considered fundamentally "muslim" (submitters to God) in their original spiritual orientation (*fitrah*), but being unique creations endowed with abilities of reason, judgment, and choice, they may remain on a God-conscious, righteous path toward divine reward, or may veer away as a consequence of upbringing and life-choices.

More commonly, the term *Muslim* refers to one who believes in the *Shahadah* (the declaration of faith containing the basic creed of Islam) and embraces a lifestyle in accord with Islamic principles and values. Anybody may be or become a Muslim, regardless of gender, race, nationality, color, or social or economic status.

Muslims Around the World

Over 1.2 billion people throughout the world are adherents of Islam. In other words, one out of every five human beings on the planet is a Muslim. Islam is the religion of diverse peoples living in Europe, Africa, the Middle East, Central, East, South and Southeast Asia, Japan, Australia, and North and South America. The global spectrum of races, ethnicities and cultures finds representation in the *ummah,* or worldwide Muslim community.

While Islam is often associated almost exclusively with the Middle East, Arabs comprise only about 15-18% of all Muslims. The country with the largest population of Muslims (over 160 million) is Indonesia, an island nation in Southeast Asia. Furthermore, the Muslim peoples of the South Asian subcontinent (living in Pakistan, India, Bangladesh, and Sri Lanka) constitute about 25% of all Muslims, while those of Africa comprise close to 20% of the total.

There are large numbers of Muslims in China (30 million) and in Iran, Egypt and Turkey (over 50 million). Moreover, Muslims constitute sizable minorities in many Western European countries, including England (over 2 million), France (over 2 million—about 10% of the French population), and Germany (about 2 million).

Muslims In the United States

An estimated six million Muslims live in North America, and of these, two and a half million are Americans who have embraced Islam (i.e., they were not born into the faith). It is projected that by the turn of the century, Islam will be the second largest religion in the United States. Even today, Muslims outnumber Episcopalians, Lutherans, Presbyterians, the United Church of Christ and many other Christian denominations, and almost as many Muslims as Jews call America their home.

There are currently more than 9,000 Muslims on active duty in the U.S. armed services. A number of leading American scientists, physicians, sports figures, and scholars are Muslim. Clearly, Muslims are part of the diverse fabric of American society, playing a productive role and sharing in the effort to make America, as well as the world, a more moral, just, and peaceful place in which to live, worship, and prosper.

Muslim Culture

Muslims throughout the world share the same essential beliefs, values, and God-centered approach to the world. Furthermore, all Muslims look to the *Qur'an* and the lifestyle and traditions of Prophet Muhammad for guidance in their daily affairs. In this respect, it may be said that Muslims share a common Islamic culture, focusing on shared principles and values.

At the same time, the ethnic, regional and material cultures of Muslims vary tremendously across the globe. Muslims exhibit different styles of clothing, different tastes for food and drink, diverse languages, and varying traditions and customs. American Muslims fall within this panorama and are in many ways culturally distinct

from Muslims living in other societal contexts. Little League base-
ball, apple pie, and jazz music are as natural to American Muslims
as they are to other Americans. Even so, certain aspects of popular
American culture (such as pre-marital relations, consumption of
alcohol, and certain styles of dress) do not accord with Islamic
principles.

Muslims view the diversity found throughout the *ummah* as a
natural part of God's plan for humanity and believe it contributes
to Islam's continued vitality and universality. Thus, rather than
imposing arbitrary cultural uniformity, Islam supports and encourages diverse cultural practices.

Basic Beliefs of Muslims

1. Allah

The central concept in Islam, reflected in the *Shahadah* (declaration of faith), is *tawheed,* or Oneness of God. For Muslims, there
is but One God who is Lord and Sovereign of Creation, and one's
devotion and obedience first of all belong to Him.

The Arabic word *Allah* is a contraction of the words "al" and
"ilah," and literally means "The God." *Allah* is the proper name for
the Creator as found in the *Qur'an.* The name *Allah* is analogous to
Eloh, a Semitic term found in the divine scriptures revealed to
Muhammad's predecessors Moses and Jesus.

The use of the term *Allah* is not confined to believers in Islam
alone—Arabic-speaking Christians and Jews also use *Allah* in ref-
erence to God, demonstrating thereby that followers of Islam, Christianity, and Judaism believe in a common monotheistic Creator. In
other words, *Allah* means "God," just as *Dios* and *Dieu* mean "God"
in Spanish and French, respectively.

The following are some verses of the *Qur'an* which describe
God and human beings' relationship with Him:

> "Say: He is God, the One, the Eternal, Absolute. He does not
> beget, nor is He begotten, and there is none like unto Him."
> (*Qur'an,* 112:1-4)

"It is He who brought you forth from the wombs of your mothers when you knew nothing, and He gave you hearing and sight and intelligence and affections that you may give thanks." (*Qur'an,* 16:78)

"No vision can grasp Him, but His grasp is over all vision. He is above all comprehension, yet is acquainted with all things." (*Qur'an,* 6:103)

Muslims believe that God has no partners or associates who share in His divinity or authority. Muslims also believe that God is transcendent and unlike His creations, and has no physical form. Nor is God believed to exist in (or be represented by) any material object. A number of divine attributes or "names," which serve to describe God, are found in the *Qur'an.* Examples of such attributes include the "Most Merciful," the "Most Forgiving," the "Most High," the "Unique," and the "Everlasting."

2. Angels

Mala'ikah, or Angels, are believed to be among God's many creations, and belief in angels is symbolic of a Muslim's belief in *al-Ghayb,* the world of the unseen (a world of which only God has knowledge). Angels are heavenly beings created by God to perform various duties.

Some angels are considered more prominent than others. *Jibreel* (Gabriel), for example, is known as the "Angel of Revelation," since he communicated God's revelations and scriptures to various human prophets and also announced to Mary, mother of Jesus, that she would bear the messiah awaited by the Children of Israel.

3. Prophets

Muslims believe that God has provided guidance to humanity over the ages through the institution of prophethood. In the Islamic context, prophets were righteous and truthful messengers selected by God to fulfill the most important mission—calling on people to worship God alone and teaching them to live righteously, in accordance with God's commandments. Essentially, prophets gave warnings as well as glad tidings to fellow human beings: warnings of punishment in this world and the next for unjust, immoral people who have turned away from God and His natural order, and glad tidings of reward in this world and the next for those who are conscious of God and follow His guidance as revealed through the prophets.

Muslims believe that God has chosen, throughout history, thousands of prophets from among all peoples of the earth. According to the *Qur'an,* prophethood ended with Muhammad (570–632 C.E.).

> "Say: We believe in Allah and that which is revealed to us, and in what was revealed to Abraham, Ishma'il, Isaac, Jacob, and the tribes, to Moses and Jesus and the other prophets from their Lord. We make no distinction between any of them, and to Allah we have surrendered ourselves." (*Qur'an,* 2: 136)

Thus, in Islam, the prophets are seen as spiritual brothers one to another. Some commonly known figures who are considered prophets include Noah, Jonah, Abraham, Ishmail, Isaac, Joseph, Moses, David, Solomon, and Jesus.

Muslims believe that Jesus was a very important prophet of God, and that he was indeed the Messiah awaited by the Jews of ancient Palestine. Like Christians, Muslims believe Jesus' mission was to reestablish justice among people and rectify deviations that had developed in the religion of the One God. Muslims share with Christians belief in Jesus' unique birth and various miracles performed by him. However, Muslims do not believe in Jesus' divinity and do not consider Jesus the "Son of God," since to do so would contradict the *Qur'anic* concept of God's Unity (Oneness).

Prophet Muhammad. Prophet Muhammad was born into the tribe of Quraysh in the city of Makkah in 570 C.E. At a very young age Muhammad experienced the loss of his parents and became an orphan. For the next few years his grandfather took care of him, followed by his uncle Abu Talib, a well-respected member of the Quraysh tribe. Muhammad grew up to become an honest and trustworthy businessman. Indeed, Muhammad's upright and dependable reputation earned him the designation *al-Amin* ("the Trustworthy One") among his fellow Makkans, and even invited a marriage proposal from Khadijah, a businesswoman in Makkah for whom Muhammad worked.

While most of his fellow Makkans were polytheists, Muhammad refused to worship the traditional tribal deities and often retreated to meditate and worship the One God of his ancestor, Abraham. In 610 C.E., while meditating in the cave of Hira in the mountains above Makkah, Muhammad received the first of many revelations, beginning with the Arabic word *Iqra,* meaning "Read" or "Recite." Soon afterward, he was commanded to convey the Divine message and thus became the last messenger of God, according to the *Qur'an.*

> "Read, in the name of thy Lord, Who Created—Created man, out of a clot (embryo). Proclaim! And thy Lord is Most Bountiful, He Who taught the use of the pen—Taught man that which he knew not." (*Qur'an,* 96: 1-5)

Muhammad spent the remaining twenty-three years of his life advocating the message of Islam among the peoples of the Arabian peninsula and working to implement the principles and teachings of Islam in human society. After suffering severe persecution from the polytheistic Makkans for 11 years, he and his fellow Muslims emigrated to Yathrib, a city 200 miles north of Makkah, where he established Islamic rule. The city was renamed *Madinah* (short for *Madinat an-Nabi,* City of the Prophet). In the following years, the message of Islam brought more and more tribes in the Arabian peninsula into the fold, creating a new community based on common religious principles, rather than tribal or other affiliations.

Islam teaches that Muhammad's role as the final prophet of God was to confirm the authentic teachings of previous prophets and to rectify mistakes or innovations that followers of previous monotheistic faith traditions had introduced into the original religion of humankind. Muhammad is also viewed as the conduit for the completion of God's guidance to humanity; the scope of his mission is seen as encompassing all people, rather than a specific region, group or community. Furthermore, his life serves as a perfect model of how to practice Islam fully.

The view of Islam as having achieved its final form through the scripture given to Muhammad and his own teachings is an important aspect of faith. Consequently, any claimants to prophethood after Muhammad, who died in 632 C.E. at the age of 63, are not accepted by Muslims.

4. Divine Scriptures

Muslims believe God revealed scriptures through the angel *Jibreel* (Gabriel) to certain prophets to communicate His commandments and guidance to humanity. For Muslims, belief in the original scriptures revealed to Abraham (Scrolls), Moses (Torah, including the Ten Commandments), David (Psalms) and Jesus (Evangelium or original Gospel) is an essential component of faith. Indeed, one cannot be considered a Muslim unless one believes in these previous scriptures and their historical role in the spiritual development of humankind.

The *Qur'an*. The word *Qur'an* literally means "the reading" or "the recitation," and is considered by Muslims to be the literal Speech of God in the Arabic language. Since Muhammad is considered the last prophet of God, the *Qur'an* is believed to be the final revelation from God to humanity. Contrary to common misconception, Muhammad is not the author of the *Qur'an*. Rather, he is viewed as the chosen transmitter of the revelation and the ideal implementer of principles and commandments contained within it. The personal sayings or words of Muhammad are known as *hadith,* which are distinct from the divine content of the *Qur'an*.

Translations of the *Qur'an* exist in many languages, including English, Spanish, French, German, Urdu, Chinese, Malay, Vietnamese, and others. While translations are useful as renderings or explanations of the *Qur'an,* only the original Arabic text is considered to be the *Qur'an* itself. As a consequence, Muslims the world over, regardless of their native language, always strive to learn Arabic, so they can read and understand the *Qur'an* in its original form.

The *Qur'an* is comprised of 114 *surahs* (chapters), arranged with the longest chapter (*al-Baqarah,* The Cow) near the beginning. Rather than presenting a sequential account of human spiritual history beginning with Adam and culminating with Muhammad, the *Qur'an*'s chapters focus on various important themes and issues, such as humans' relationship with God, God's unique attributes, human accountability and the Day of Judgment, ethics, social justice, politics, the rise and fall of nations, law, the natural world and family issues. The *Qur'an* stresses the development of certain moral and spiritual characteristics, and links these with establishing justice and righteousness in the world. Many of the lessons of the *Qur'an* are given through accounts of past prophets and peoples.

5. Day of Judgment

Muslims believe that one's essential purpose in this world is to recognize and serve God by implementing His guidance as found in His divine scriptures and in the teachings of the prophets.

Islam teaches that human beings are responsible to God for all their words and deeds. The relatively short span of our lives, therefore, constitutes a test.

"He is the one who created death and life that He may test which of you is best in deeds" (*Qur'an,* 67:2).

In the interest of justice and to fulfill God's divine plan, a day will come when the present world will be destroyed and the entire human race will be resurrected and assembled before God for individual judgment. Each person will either be rewarded with permanent bliss in *Jannah* (Heaven) or be punished with suffering in *Jahannam* (Hell). The infinite mercy of God is evident in the Qur'anic statement that those who have even a mustard seed's weight of belief in God will eventually be admitted into Heaven.

Related Issues

Depictions of Religious Figures

Muslims do not possess pictures or depictions of any of the prophets, or even of the companions of Prophet Muhammad. Nor are pictures of persons, animals or heavenly figures part of the Islamic religious tradition. One reason for this is that the accuracy of such pictures would be questionable, especially for older religious figures like Jesus, Moses or Abraham. Furthermore, Muslims believe it is not inconceivable that over time, highly revered persons represented visually could acquire an aura of divinity. Muslims are extremely wary of any practices which may lead to *shirk*, or ascribing divinity to anyone or anything in conjunction with God.

Historically, the cautionary ethos of Islam regarding representational art mainly applied to subjects of a religious nature. Outside the realm of the sacred, many artists and artisans created paintings, ceramics and other items containing depictions of humans, animals and other figures. Even so, the majority of Muslim artistic expression has revolved around geometric and vegetal designs or calligraphic representation of the *Qur'an.*

Men and Women In Islam

According to Islam, men and women are spiritually equal beings created from a common origin. All of the religious obligations in Islam are incumbent upon both women and men, such as daily worship, fasting, performing the *Hajj,* etc. God's mercy and forgiveness apply equally to men and women. The following *Qur'anic* verse illustrates this point:

"For Muslim men and Muslim women,
For believing men and believing women,
For devout men and devout women,
For true men and true women,
For men and women who are patient and constant,
For men and women who humble themselves,
For men and women who give in charity,

For men and women who fast,
For men and women who guard their chastity,
And for men and women who engage much in God's praise,
For them has God prepared forgiveness and great reward."
(*Qur'an*, 33:35)

As a consequence of physiological, psychological and other distinguishing factors embodied in men and women by the Creator, the rights, responsibilities, and roles of men and women are believed to naturally differ. Muslims believe that God has assigned the responsibility of providing financially for the family to men, and the important responsibility of nurturing a God-conscious and righteous family to women. Such roles do not preclude women from having careers and earning income or men from helping to raise a family. Rather they provide a general framework for Muslim society, designed to reinforce the concept of a nuclear family unit.

The *Qur'an* specifies the natural and inherent rights of women as well as men, and enjoins people to act in line with God's teachings of justice and equity. Some of the rights of women elaborated in the *Qur'an* and *Sunnah* include the right to own and inherit property, the right to obtain an education, the right to contract marriage and seek divorce, the right to retain one's family name upon marriage, the right to vote and express opinions on societal affairs, and the right to be supported financially by male relatives (husband, father, brother, etc.). Such rights were unheard of in the seventh century, yet were implemented to varying degrees in Muslim civilization throughout the last fourteen hundred years. Thus, common stereotypes regarding women's rights must be carefully considered, and the current practice of Muslims in various countries and regions, as well as prevailing cultural factors, must be examined within the context of history and within light of the sources of Islam in order to ascertain the degree to which Muslim women are able to exercise their rights today.

Dietary Issues

In the *Qur'an*, very few foods are expressly forbidden. The most important items prohibited are pork and its by-products, and meat of animals slaughtered in the name of anything other than the One God. When Muslims slaughter animals for consumption, they pronounce the name of God during the act, symbolizing recognition of His bounty and His role as Creator of all things. Such blessed meat is termed *halal,* a designation similar to "kosher" used by Jews. In fact, the *Qur'an* states that meat from the *Ahl al-Kitab,* or "People of the Book" (Christians and Jews) is permissible for Muslims to eat. Such legal provisions serve to reiterate the common monotheistic bond of the three Abrahamic religions (religions that recognize Abraham as a prophet). At the same time, many Muslims do not eat meat from commercial sources, since rules for slaughtering animals in Islam differ from those current in America.

Substances which are detrimental to human health or livelihood are also prohibited. Chief among these is alcohol, since it alters one's mental state and impairs one's abilities for reasoning and judgment, affects one's moral compass, and interferes with the proper functioning of the biological senses. So-called recreational drugs such as cocaine, heroine, and marijuana are also prohibited.

Mild stimulants such as caffeine found in chocolate, coffee, tea and soft drinks are not deemed to have direly adverse effects, and therefore are permissible, so long as one does not feel addicted to them. Some scholars view smoking as *haram,* due to its addictive nature and clearly detrimental effects upon a person's health and well-being.

Manner of Dress

From the Islamic perspective, clothes are meant for cover and simple adornment, not for demonstration of social status or attraction of the opposite sex. In other words, guidelines for dress are meant to prevent men and women from being objects of desire and temptation. Islamic dress is based on a few guidelines: clothes should be loose fitting, such that the shape of the body is not highlighted; clothes should not be transparent or sheer; clothes should cover certain prescribed parts of the body—for men, minimally from the navel to the knee (though it is extremely rare to see a male in a Muslim setting who isn't covered from ankle to neck), and for women, everything except for face, hands and feet. Muslim women who cover according to these guidelines are said to be in *hijab*. The term is also used commonly to describe the head covering or scarf worn by many Muslim women.

In practice, Muslim peoples have integrated the Islamic dress requirements with their own local cultures, customs and geographical conditions, resulting in great varieties of clothing and styles. In the United States, Muslims may be seen wearing Western styles adapted to Islamic requirements of modesty.

Nation of Islam

The Nation of Islam was founded in the 1930s by Elijah Poole, who later became widely known as Elijah Muhammad. The organization was formed to address the civil rights concerns of African-Americans in the United States, and advocated complete segregation from "white" society. In order to rally the support of African-Americans seeking an alternative to traditional approaches to long-standing injustices, the Nation used terminology borrowed from the religion of Islam, and simultaneously developed an elaborate mythology to support its claims of black racial superiority.

After the death of Elijah Muhammad in 1975, his son Warith Deen Muhammad renounced the race-based teachings of the Nation. He and his followers then joined the mainstream community of Muslims. The Nation was later revived by Louis Farrakhan. Today, according to a study by Numan and Associates (Washington DC) there are less than 10,000 followers of Farrakhan.

Because the Nation holds that Elijah Muhammad was a prophet of God and that his mentor W.D. Fard was God Incarnate, the Nation cannot be considered a branch or subset of Islam by mainstream Muslims. Such beliefs are contrary to the basic doctrines and tenets of Islam as defined in the *Qur'an* and *Sunnah*. Furthermore, the race-based orientation of the Nation contradicts the universalist outlook advocated by worldwide Islam.

The term "Black Muslim" has been used to describe a follower of the Nation of Islam, though it is considered a confusing misnomer by mainstream Muslims, since Islam is practiced by people of every race and ethnicity. For Muslims the term "Black Muslim" is no more valid than "White Muslim."

Jihad

The Arabic word *jihad* means "struggle" or "exertion" and refers to any spiritual, moral or physical struggle. Upon returning from a battle, the Prophet Muhammad is reported to have said, "We are returning from the lesser *jihad* to the greater *jihad—jihad* against the self." For Muslims, *jihad* means struggle in the cause of God, which can take many forms. In the personal sphere, efforts such as obtaining an education, trying to quit smoking, or controlling one's temper are forms of *jihad.*

Jihad as a military action is justified in two cases: struggle to defend oneself, or others, from aggression and struggle for freedom of religion and justice. The *Qur'an* says, "Tumult and oppression are worse than killing" (2:217) and therefore must be thwarted. Human beings as responsible agents of God on earth are compelled to exert themselves to protect the oppressed and strive to create righteous societies.

Contrary to common misconceptions, *jihad* can never mean forcibly converting others to Islam, for "There is no compulsion in religion" (*Qur'an,* 2:256). Because *jihad* is a highly nuanced concept, and because the term stems from an Arabic root meaning "struggle," the term "holy war" is an inappropriate rendering or definition.

Social Justice

According to Islam, human beings are the noblest creations of God, endowed with consciousness and freedom of choice. The *Qur'an* states that God has made human beings His trustees or stewards on the earth. Muslims see this world as God's field, and human beings as the farmers and caretakers. Muslims believe humanity's ultimate task is to build a world that reflects the will of God. Thus, Islam is balanced in its concern for salvation in the Hereafter as well as peace and justice in the present world. Islam places great emphasis on social justice for all people. Muslims consider it an obligation to oppose all who exploit, oppress, discriminate, and deal unjustly with people.

"O you who believe, be upholders of justice, witnesses for God even if it be against yourselves." (*Qur'an,* 4: 135)

Muslims understand the goal of Islam to be the spiritual uplift-ment of the individual and productive development of society. The ultimate consequence of rejecting God and His guidance is a self-ish, pleasure-seeking, corrupt, and unjust society. Conversely, the natural consequence of obedience to God's laws and living accord-ing to His guidance is a society of peace, equality, freedom from want, dignity for all, and justice.

QUESTIONS AND ANSWERS

1. What defines affiliation with your religious tradition?

The most basic definition of a Muslim is one who believes in the *Shahadah,* namely, that there is no deity except the One God and Muhammad is His last prophet. Beyond belief in this creed, the effort to perform the basic acts of worship, *salah* (formal worship), *sawm* (fasting), *zakah* (alms tax) and *Hajj* (pilgrimage) is essential in demonstrating sincere affiliation with the religion of Islam.

While these acts involve specific practices and statements, Islam does not teach blind, ritualistic imitation. Muslims believe that God does not want from His servants absent-minded move-ment of the tongue and body—rather, He wants attention of the heart and sincere actions. Consequently, the *neeyah,* or intention that one has while fulfilling a particular obligation, counts a great deal. Indeed, a hadith states that "Actions are judged according to their intentions."

2. What are the major holidays of your faith tradition and what does each represent?

There are two major holidays in Islam. *Eid al-Fitr* takes place on the 1st of Shawwal, the tenth month of the Islamic lunar year, at the conclusion of *Ramadan,* the month of fasting. The holiday cele-bration begins early in the morning with a special congregational worship. The *Eid* prayers are often held in a specially designated gathering place, such as a park or convention center, meant to accommodate large numbers of Muslims from several local *masjids*.

After the prayer, the *imam* (worship leader) delivers a short *khutbah* (sermon or address). Then all rise to their feet to greet and hug one another. The rest of the festival's observances are held among family and friends, and include visits, shared meals, new clothes, gifts for young children, and lots of sweets. In Muslim countries, festivities are often in evidence for three or more days. In order to share the spirit of the occasion with all members of society, Muslims pay a special nominal charity tax which is used to purchase food, clothing and gifts for needy persons.

Eid al-Adha takes place on the tenth of *Dhul-Hijjah* (the twelfth month of the Islamic lunar calendar), after the majority of *Hajj* rituals are completed by pilgrims. Around the world, Muslims share in the spirit of the *Hajj* by observing the *Eid* festivities in their own localities. The day's observances are similar to those of *Eid al-Fitr,* with the addition of a special sacrifice—Muslims commemorate Prophet Abraham's willingness to sacrifice his elder son Ishma'il when God commanded him to do so as a test of his commitment. Since God miraculously provided a lamb to Abraham which took the place of his son, Muslims recall the event by sacrificing animals such as lambs, goats, sheep, cows or camels. The sacrifice may be performed any time after the *Eid* morning prayers until the evening of the twelfth of *Dhul-Hijjah.* The meat of the sacrificed animals is distributed to the poor or needy, and portions are kept for one's own family and friends during this time of extra charity and hospitality.

3. What are the rituals of your tradition that surround the rites of passage?

There are no official sacraments or rites of passage in Islam. However, the *Shari'ah* (Islamic Law) indicates that a Muslim becomes fully accountable to God for his or her actions at the age of puberty. This sense of accountability is evident in the training younger Muslims engage in before becoming adults, though no official ceremony marks passage into adulthood.

Even so, a number of traditional rituals are practiced by some Muslims in honor of children. For example, soon after birth a newborn's father whispers the *adhan* (call to prayer) into his or her ears. This act signifies that the child has been born into a community centered around prayer and worship of the Creator.

Another common tradition is the *aqiqah,* in which the birth-hair of the newborn girl or boy is shaved off to signify a new phase of life outside the womb. The *aqiqah* is usually performed on the seventh day after birth, though it may be done later. In addition, a goat or lamb is typically sacrificed for a feast of thanksgiving. During the feast, family and friends pray that God blesses the child with good health and happiness and protects her or him from all physical harm and evil influences.

After birth or in early childhood, male children are circumcised in accordance with the *Sunnah.* The circumcision may be seen as a symbolic act, performed in homage to the great sacrifices to which Prophet Abraham and his son were committed. Circumcision may also reiterate Muslims' view of Islam as a continual message unfolded through history, since the practice is found among Jews, descendants of the followers of the earlier prophet Moses. Circumcision is not obligatory upon adult converts, since it is not a strict requirement of *Shari'ah.* Moreover, female circumcision is contrary to the most basic teachings of Islam, and finds no sanction in Islamic Law.

If anything, accumulation of knowledge is the measure of "passage" or growth in Islam. The *Qur'an* repeatedly reminds readers that "those who know" are not the same as "those who know not," and a *hadith* of Prophet Muhammad states that seeking knowledge is an obligation for both men and women. Consequently, most Muslim parents tend to be very involved in their children's education. Teachers are highly respected and are seen as allies in cultivating knowledge and in presenting positive role models for students.

Naturally, religious education is very important to Muslims. At an early age, children begin memorizing the short verses of the *Qur'an,* especially *al-Fatihah,* the opening chapter. In some Muslim cultures, around the age of four, a *Bismillah* ceremony is held to signify a child's readiness to begin learning to read the *Qur'an* in Arabic. This tradition, while not a part of the *Sunnah,* is very common among Muslims of the Indian subcontinent (Pakistan, India, Bangladesh, Sri Lanka), Southeast Asia (Indonesia, Malaysia) and Central Asia. Some time later, when the child has completed his or her first full reading of the entire *Qur'an*, an *Ameen* ceremony is held. The *Ameen*, like the *Bismillah* event, is not a religious obligation and is a tradition among some Muslims meant to celebrate a child's reading of the *Qur'an*.

4. Does your tradition have a view of afterlife? If so, describe it briefly.

Muslims believe that death is not the end of life, but rather a transitory state. After death, life continues in a different form. Various verses in the *Qur'an* describe Heaven as a place of blissful gardens and rivers, where all of one's desires may be fulfilled, while Hell is described as a place of fire and torment. Some scholars believe that such descriptions are in part allegorical, and serve to provide in human terms a symbol for the experience of the Hereafter. Even so, no matter what form they take, physical or ethereal, reward and punishment are considered patently real by Muslims.

5. What are the regular personal obligations and worship patterns of your faith's community?

Every action performed in obedience to God's guidance or in order to please Him is considered an act of *ibadah* (worship) in Islam. Thus, helping someone with homework, greeting a stranger, and even hugging one's spouse are all acts of worship which earn spiritual reward. However, it is the specific acts of worship commonly termed the **"Five Pillars of Islam"** that provide the framework for the Muslim's spiritual life.

1. Shahadah—Declaration of Faith. The *shahadah* represents the first pillar of Islam, upon which everything else is based. The *shahadah* is a twofold declaration or statement—it is a denial of any *thing's* worthiness for worship save God, and an affirmation of Muhammad's prophethood (and thereby the prophethood of all previous prophets, since Muhammad is considered the last). The *shahadah* states "I bear witness that there is no deity except Allah (God), and that Muhammad is His Servant and Messenger." Making the declaration in sincerity formally brings a person into the fold of Islam.

2. Salah—Formal Worship. *Salah* or formal ritual worship, is the second pillar of Islam. Muslims are required to perform *salah* five times daily—at dawn, midday, in the afternoon, after sunset, and at night. When the time for *salah* has arrived, a designated person called the *mueddhin* calls believers to assemble for worship. The call to prayer is called the *adhan*.

Salah is the foremost act of worship, for in the various movements of the worship act, a symbolic submission to God can be discerned. An important component of *salah* is the recitation of verses from the *Qur'an*. Worshipers recite *al-Fatihah,* the opening chapter of the scripture, as well as other verses of their choice from memory. The *salah* also entails various supplications for God's mercy and blessings, and various statements glorifying God.

> **The Opening Chapter of the Qur'an (*al-Fatihah*):**
> "Praise be to God, the Cherisher and Sustainer of the Worlds
> Most Gracious, Most Merciful
> Master of the Day of Judgement
> You do we worship, and Your aid we seek
> Show us the straight way,
> The way of those on whom You have bestowed Your Mercy
> Of those who do not earn Your anger, nor go astray."
> (*Qur'an*, 1:1-7)

Salah reinforces God-consciousness, thereby reducing the likelihood of disobeying God and committing sins. *Salah* also provides a respite from the day's challenges and circumstances, enabling a believer to refresh his or her intimate, personal relationship with God. Typically, after completing the formal worship, Muslims engage in *du'a,* or personal prayer, in which they may thank God for His blessings and pray for forgiveness, good health, prosperity, happiness, assistance in times of distress, or anything one may desire.

3. Sawm—Fasting. The *Qur'an* enjoins Muslims to fast as a means of demonstrating commitment to God in the face of temptation and difficulty. *Sawm*, fasting from dawn to sunset during the month of *Ramadan*, means not eating any foods, drinking any beverages (including water), or engaging in marital sexual relations from dawn to sunset. On the spiritual and moral level, it means struggling to develop self-restraint, God-consciousness and piety. Moreover, *sawm* puts into perspective the plight of those unable to obtain regular nourishing meals. Muslims strive in this month to curb all detrimental desires and negative or uncharitable thoughts, and to nurture love, patience, unselfishness and social consciousness. When fasting, Muslims often discover a calm, inner peace which helps them become even closer to God.

4. Zakah—Mandatory Almsgiving Tax. *Zakah* is an act of worship in which eligible Muslims pay a specified amount of money (about 2.5% of one's accumulated wealth) as a tax to be used to assist poor and needy persons in society. The annual payment of *zakah* "purifies" one's income and wealth by reminding Muslims that their possessions are in reality a trust and a test from God, to be used not only for personal benefit, but for the benefit of others as well. Thus, paying the *zakah* is a means of earning spiritual reward from God and divine reimbursement in the Hereafter. Conversely, neglecting to pay *zakah* is a grievous sin.

On a societal level, *Zakah* helps to establish economic justice, by maintaining a minimal standard of living for the least fortunate members of society.

5. Hajj—Pilgrimage to Makkah. Muslims are required to perform the *Hajj*, or pilgrimage to Makkah, at least once in their lifetime if they are physically and financially able to do so. *Hajj* is a time of turning away from the world in order to turn toward God and sincerely seek His forgiveness for past sins and errors. The rites of the *Hajj* commemorate the trials and sacrifices of Prophet Abraham, his wife Hajar, and their son Prophet Ishma'il. The city of Makkah, in modern-day Saudi Arabia, is the site of the pilgrimage because the *Ka'bah*, which was built by Abraham and Ishma'il as the first "house of worship" dedicated to the One God, is located there. The *Hajj* takes place over several days in the early part of the twelfth month in the Islamic calendar, called *Dhul-Hijjah.*

Every year, over two million Muslims from all over the world, comprising the largest annual international gathering on earth, perform the *Hajj* rites. Upon approaching the holy land, pilgrims enter a state of consecration (solemn dedication) known as *ihram,* and don the *ihram* attire, comprised of several sheets of white, unstitched, seamless cloth. Donning the *ihram* symbolizes for a Muslim the leaving behind of the material world for the sake of God, and also reminds him or her of his or her mortality, since the white cloth evokes the image of the death shroud Muslims use to wrap the deceased. The collective sea of white created by millions of pilgrims also serves to reinforce Islam's egalitarian and universal ethos, reminding Muslims that all people are created as spiritual equals, and that only faith in God and righteousness in this life differentiates one from another.

6. What are your religion's views about revelation and the source(s) of religious authority?

The concept of revelation is central to Islam, for it is the mechanism through which human beings learn of God's guidance and divine plan. Belief in successive revelations, culminating with the *Qur'an,* is integral to Muslims. As the *Qur'an* is considered the literal Speech of God, it serves as the first source for Islamic doctrine, law and practice. The second source of authority is the *Sunnah,* the words and deeds of Prophet Muhammad. *Hadith* are one kind of written record of the Prophet's *Sunnah.* For *Shi'ah* Muslims, the teachings and writings of a number of early charismatic leaders called *Imams,* descended from the Prophet's son-in-law Ali, are an additional source of authority.

Muslim scholars use these sources in order to understand and explain doctrine, and determine the principles of *Shari'ah* (Islamic Law) contained in them, in order to develop legal opinions on existent as well as novel situations faced by the Muslim community. The authentic sources also serve as criteria for differentiating between religiously-based actions or opinions and those resulting from other factors, such as culture, social status or circumstance.

The use of terms such as "priesthood" or "clergy" to describe Muslim religious leaders is inappropriate. In Islam, religious leaders or scholars are not ordained persons, nor do they belong to any kind of leadership hierarchy. Rather, they are simply individual Muslims who have acquired more religious knowledge than the average believer. While such persons play valuable religious and social roles within the community, it is important to note that they do not in any way serve as spiritual *intercessors* between individual Muslims and God. Moreover, each believer is personally responsible for his or her own actions and beliefs, and is not bound by any given scholarly opinion on various issues. The sources of Islam, especially the *Qur'an,* are considered to be directly accessible to individual Muslims.

7. What is your faith's view of salvation?

For Muslims, belief in the Oneness of God is paramount, and eclipses all other factors in determining one's final destination. Furthermore, following the straight path laid down by the prophets and exemplified by Prophet Muhammad demonstrates commitment to God's commandments and guidance, ensuring God's love and mercy on the Day of Judgment. Another factor in one's spiritual life is repentance for past sins. Muslims believe that God forgives those who repent in sincerity and who strive (*jihad*) to better themselves in all respects.

Furthermore, Muslims do not believe in "Original Sin," the concept that the sin of Adam is inherited by all humankind. Rather, Muslims believe that each person is personally accountable to God, and will be judged by Him according to their good and bad deeds, independent of those of others. Ultimately, the Creator is the sole judge, and Muslims believe that no human being can judge another in spiritual terms. The Day of Judgment signals the end of the present order of things, in which human beings are tested in their commitment to God. In Islamic terms, "salvation" means successfully meeting the challenges of the temporary earthly life and earning eternal reward and nearness to God in the Hereafter.

GLOSSARY OF TERMS

Adhan [ad-HAAN]. The Muslim call to worship, consisting of specific Arabic phrases, recited aloud by a *mueddhin* (caller) prior to each of the five daily worship times. Upon hearing the *adhan,* Muslims assemble for formal communal worship.

Ahl al-Kitab [AHL al-kee-TAAB]. Literally, "People of the Book." This term, found in the *Qur'an,* describes adherents of divinely revealed religions that preceded Islam. Most commonly, the term refers to Jews and Christians, and historically conferred upon them a special status within Muslim society, owing to the monotheistic basis of their religions.

Allah [al-LAH]. Literally, "The God." Muslims use this Arabic term as the proper name for God. Muslims view *Allah* as the Creator and Sustainer of everything in the universe, who is transcendent, has no physical form, and has no associates who share in His divinity.

(al-) Aqsa [al-UCK-sa]. Name of the holy site located in the city of Jerusalem and referred to in the *Qur'an* as "the farthest *masjid.*" The site is believed to be the area from which Prophet Muhammad was miraculously ascended to Heaven in 619 C.E.

"As-Salaam Alaykum." The traditional greeting of Muslims, meaning "Peace be upon you." The appropriate response is *"Wa Alaykum As-Salaam,"* meaning, "And upon you be peace also."

Day of Judgment. Muslims believe that after God ends the present world and order of creation, a day will follow on which He will judge each person according to his or her intentions, deeds, and circumstances. Judgment by God is followed by punishment in Hell or eternal reward in Heaven.

Eid [EED]. *Eid* is an Arabic term meaning "festivity" or "celebration." Muslims celebrate two major religious holidays, known as *Eid al-Fitr* (which takes place after *Ramadan*), and *Eid al-Adha* (which occurs at the time of the *Hajj*). A special congregational *Eid* worship, visitation of family and friends, new clothing, specially-prepared foods and sweets, and gifts for children characterize these holidays.

Fitrah [FIT-rah]. An Arabic term designating the innate, original spiritual orientation of every human being toward God the Creator. Muslims believe that God endowed everything in Creation with a tendency toward goodness, piety and God-consciousness, and that one's environment, upbringing, and circumstances serve to enhance or obscure this tendency.

Hadith [ha-DEETH]. Unlike the text of the *Qur'an, Hadith* are the sayings and traditions of Prophet Muhammad himself, and form part of the record of the Prophet's *Sunnah* (way of life and example). The *Hadith,* found in various collections compiled by Muslim scholars in the early centuries of the Muslim civilization, are a source of guidance for many aspects of life.

Hajj [HUJ]. The pilgrimage (journey) to Makkah (in modern-day Saudi Arabia) undertaken by Muslims in commemoration of the Abrahamic roots of Islam. The *Hajj* rites symbolically reenact the trials and sacrifices of Prophet Abraham, his wife Hajar, and their son Ishma'il over 4,000 years ago. Muslims must perform the *Hajj* at least once in their lives, provided their health permits and they are financially capable. The *Hajj* is performed annually by over 2,000,000 people during the twelfth month of the Islamic lunar calendar, *Dhul-Hijjah.*

Hijrah [HIJ-rah]. The migration in 622 C.E. of Prophet Muhammad and members of the Muslim community from the city of Makkah to the city of Yathrib, later renamed Madinah an-Nabi (city of the Prophet) in honor of Muhammad. The Islamic lunar calendar, often called the *Hijri* calendar, is dated from this important event, which marks the beginning of an Islamic state (in Madinah) in which the *Shari'ah* (Islamic Law) was implemented.

Imam [ee-MAAM]. Generally, the term *imam* refers to one who leads congregational worship. More broadly, the term also applies to religious leaders within the Muslim community. While *imams* lead worship, give sermons, and perform other duties such as officiating at marriages, they are not ordained clergy, nor do they belong to any kind of hierarchy. Also, *imams* do not act as intermediaries between individual worshipers and God.

Islam [iss-LAAM]. *Islam* is an Arabic word derived from the three-letter root *s-l-m*. Its meaning encompasses the concepts of peace, greeting, surrender, and commitment, and refers commonly to an individual's surrender and commitment to God the Creator through adherence to the religion by the same name.

Jibreel [jib-REEL]. *Jibreel* (Gabriel) is believed to be one of the most important angels, as he was responsible for transmitting God's divine revelations to all of the human prophets, ending with Muhammad.

Jihad [ji-HAAD]. *Jihad* is an Arabic word which means "to exert oneself" or "to strive." Other meanings include endeavor, diligence, and struggle. Usually understood in terms of personal betterment, *jihad* may also mean fighting to defend one's (or another's) life, property, and faith. Because *jihad* is a highly nuanced concept, it should not be understood to mean "holy war," a common mis-representation.

Ka'bah [KA-bah]. An empty cube-shaped structure located in the city of Makkah (in modern-day Saudi Arabia). Built by Prophet Abraham and his son Prophet Ishma'il about 4,000 years ago, the *Ka'bah* stands as the first building dedicated to the worship of the One God. The *Ka'bah* is made of stone, and is covered by a black and gold cloth embroidered with verses from the *Qur'an.*

Khalifah [kha-LEE-fah]. An Arabic term meaning "successor," it refers to the rightful successor of Prophet Muhammad as leader of the *ummah* (worldwide Muslim community). The *Khalifah* (caliph) is not a prophet; rather, he is charged with upholding the rights of all citizens within an Islamic state and ensuring application of the *Shari'ah* (Islamic Law). The immediate successors of Prophet Muhammad, known as the "Rightly-Guided" Caliphs, were Abu Bakr as-Sadiq, Umar ibn al-Khattab, Uthman ibn Affan, and Ali ibn Abi Talib.

Madinah [ma-DEE-nah]. Formerly named Yathrib, Madinah became the center of the first Islamic community and political state after Prophet Muhammad migrated there from Makkah in 622 C.E. The people of Madinah welcomed the persecuted Muslims of Makkah with open arms, establishing a sense of brother-hood and sisterhood viewed as a tangible ideal for Muslims today. Prophet Muhammad died in Madinah in 632 C.E. and was buried in his room adjacent to the city's central *masjid*, which he established.

Makkah [MUCK-ah]. An ancient city where Abraham and Ishma'il built the *Ka'bah*. Muhammad, a member of the Quraysh tribe, which traced its lineage back to Abraham, was born in Makkah in 570 C.E. After migrating to Madinah to further the message of Islam, Muhammad returned to Makkah in 629 C.E. with fellow Muslims to reinstitute the age-old monotheistic *Hajj*. In 630 C.E., after the Quraysh violated a peace treaty, Muhammad marched on Makkah and gained control of the city peacefully, thereafter clearing the *Ka'bah* of idols and reintegrating the city into the fold of Islam.

Mala'ikah [ma-LAA-ik-ah]. Angels, a class of God's creations. Angels inhabit the unseen world, and constitute a group of beings who do God's bidding and who perpetually engage in His glorification. Muslims believe each human being is assigned two special angels as recorders—one records a person's good deeds while the other records a person's evil deeds. These records will be summoned on the Day of Judgment and each individual will be called to account for his or her deeds.

Masjid [MUS-jid]. A term meaning "place of prostration," *masjid* designates a building where Muslims congregate for communal worship. The term comes from the same Arabic root as the word *sujud,* designating the important worship position in which Muslims touch their forehead to the ground. Often, the French word *mosque* is used interchangeably with *masjid,* though the latter term is preferred by Muslims. The *masjid* also serves various social, educational, and religious purposes.

Muhammad [moo-HUM-mud]. The prophet and righteous person believed by Muslims to be the final messenger of God, whose predecessors are believed to include the Prophets Adam, Noah, Abraham, Moses, David, Jesus and others. Born in 570 C.E., Muhammad grew up to become a well-respected member of Makkan society. In 610 C.E., he received the first of many revelations that would eventually form the content of the *Qur'an*. Soon after this initial event, he was conferred prophethood and began calling people to righteousness and belief in One God. Muhammad died in 632 C.E., after successfully (re)establishing the religion known as Islam and providing Muslims with a model for ideal human behavior.

Muslim [MOOS-lim]. Literally (and in the broadest sense), the term means "one who submits to God." More commonly, the term describes any person who accepts the creed and the teachings of Islam. The word "Muhammadan" is a pejorative and offensive misnomer, as it violates Muslims' most basic understanding of their creed—Muslims do not worship Muhammad, nor do they view him as the founder of the religion. The word "Moslem" is also incorrect, since it is a corruption of the word "Muslim."

Qur'an [QOOR-aan]. The word *Qur'an* means "the recitation" or "the reading," and refers to the divinely revealed scripture of Islam. It consists of 114 *surahs* (chapters) revealed by God to Muhammad over a period of twenty-three years. The *Qur'an* continues to be recited by Muslims throughout the world in the language of its revelation, Arabic, exactly as it was recited by Prophet Muhammad nearly fourteen hundred years ago. The *Qur'an* is viewed as the authoritative guide for human beings, along with the *Sunnah* of Muhammad. Translations of the *Qur'an* are considered explanations of the meaning of the *Qur'an*, but not the *Qur'an* itself. The spelling "Koran" is phonetically incorrect; the more accurate *Qur'an* should be used.

Ramadan [ra-ma-DAAN]. The ninth month of the Islamic lunar calendar, *Ramadan* is important because it is the month in which the first verses of the *Qur'an* were revealed to Muhammad. Furthermore, *Ramadan* is the month in which Muslims fast daily from dawn to sunset to develop piety and self-restraint.

Salah [sa-LAAH]. *Salah* refers to the prescribed form of worship in Islam, and is one of the "five pillars" of Islam. Muslims perform the *salah* five times throughout each day as a means of maintaining God-consciousness, to thank Him for His blessings and bounty, and to seek His assistance and support in one's daily life.

Sawm [SO-um]. *Sawm* refers to the daily fast Muslims undertake during the month of *Ramadan,* and is one of the "five pillars" of Islam. For Muslims, fasting means total abstinence from all food, drink, and marital sexual relations from dawn to sunset. Muslims fast for many reasons, including to build a sense of willpower against temptation, to feel compassion for less fortunate persons, and to reevaluate their lives in spiritual terms.

Shahadah [sha-HAA-duh]. An Arabic word meaning "witnessing," *Shahadah* refers to the declaration of faith (*"La-Ilaha-Illa-Lah Muhammadur-Rasul-Allah"*) which all Muslims take as their creed— namely, that there is no deity but God and that Muhammad is the Messenger of God. The *Shahadah* constitutes the first of the "five pillars" of Islam.

Shari'ah [sha-REE-ah]. Literally "the path," this term refers to guidance from God to be used by Muslims to regulate their societal and personal affairs. The *Shari'ah* is based upon the *Qur'an* and the *Sunnah* of Muhammad, and is interpreted by scholars in deliberating and deciding upon questions and issues of a legal nature.

Shi'ism [SHEE-ism]. A branch of Islam comprising about 10% of the total Muslim population. *Shi'ahs* (believers in *Shi'ism*) hold that Ali ibn Abi Talib was the rightful successor to Prophet Muhammad. Moreover, *Shi'ahs* believe that Ali was granted a unique spiritual authority, which was passed on to certain of his descendants given the title of *Imam* (leader). The largest group in *Shi'ism* believes that Ali was the first of twelve *Imams,* and that the last one continues to exist, albeit miraculously and in a state of occultation (concealment from human view). The teachings of these spiritual leaders are an additional source of *Shari'ah* (Islamic Law), used by *Shi'i* religious scholars.

Sunnah [SOON-nah]. Literally, this term means practice, customary procedure, action, or usage sanctioned by tradition. More specifically, *Sunnah* refers to Prophet Muhammad's sayings, practices, and habits. The *Hadith* of the Prophet constitute a written record of his *Sunnah.*

Sunni [SOON-nee]. A term designating those Muslims who recognize the first four successors of Prophet Muhammad as the "Rightly-Guided" caliphs. *Sunnis* hold that any pious, just, and qualified Muslim may be elected caliph. *Sunnis* comprise the majority of Muslims, numbering about 90% of the total.

Surah [SOO-rah]. A distinct chapter of the *Qur'an,* designated by a title such as *Abraham, The Pilgrimage,* or *The Table-Spread.* An individual verse within a *surah* is called an *ayah.* The *Qur'an* is comprised of 114 *surahs* of varying lengths.

Ummah [OOM-mah]. The worldwide community of Muslims, whose population exceeds 1.2 billion. A term used to denote the collective body of believers in Islam.

Zakah [za-KAAH]. *Zakah* literally means "purification," and refers to an almsgiving tax, roughly 2.5% of one's wealth, that eligible Muslims pay annually. *Zakah* is one of the "five pillars" of Islam, and is usually collected by local *masjids* or charitable organizations. The funds are distributed to poor and needy persons in the Muslim community.

SUGGESTED READING

For Teachers:

Ahmed, Akbar. *Living Islam: From Samarkand to Stornoway.* Facts on File, 1992. ISBN: 0-8160-1303-7

Ali, Abdullah Yusuf, tr. *The Meaning of the Holy Qur'an.* American Trust Publications, 1983. ISBN: 0-89259-006-8

al-Faruqi, Isma'il. *Islam.* International Graphics, 1984. ISBN: 0-89505-022-6

al-Faruqi, Lois Lamya. *Women, Muslim Society, and Islam.* American Trust Publications, 1991. ISBN: 0-89259-068-8

al-Sahrawardy, Allama Sir Abdullah. *The Sayings of Muhammad.* Citadel Press, 1990. ISBN: 0-8065-01169-9

Armstrong, Karen. *Muhammad: A Biography of the Prophet.* Harper-Collins, 1992. ISBN: 0-06-250886-5

Asad, Muhammad, tr. *The Message of the Qur'an*. Dar al-Andalus, 1980. ISBN: 0-317-5245-9

Cleary, Thomas. *The Wisdom of the Prophet—Sayings of Muhammad*. Shambala Press, 1994. ISBN: 1-57062-017-2

Teaching About Islam and Muslims in the Public School Classroom. Council on Islamic Education, 1992.

Esposito, John. *Islam—The Straight Path*. Oxford University Press, 1988. ISBN: 0-19-504399-5

Glassé, Cyril. *The Concise Encyclopedia of Islam*. HarperCollins, 1989. ISBN: 0-06-063126-0

Hayes, John R., ed. *The Genius of Arab Civilization: Source of Renaissance*. MIT Press, 1983. ISBN: 0-262-58063-2

Lings, Martin. *Muhammad: His Life Based on the Earliest Sources*. Inner Traditions Intl., 1983. ISBN: 0-89281-170-6

Matar, N.I. *Islam for Beginners*. Writers and Readers Publishing, 1992. ISBN: 0-86316-155-3

Nasr, Seyyed Hussein. *Science and Civilization in Islam*. Islamic Texts Society, 1987. ISBN: 0-946621-11-X

Said, Edward. *Orientalism*. Random House, 1978. ISBN: 0-394-74067-X

Wudud-Mohsin, Amina. *Qur'an and Woman*. Penerbrit Fajar Bakti, 1992. ISBN: 967-65-1976-6

For Students:

Asad, Muhammad. *The Road to Mecca*. Dar al-Andalus, 1980.

Barboza, Steven. *American Jihad—Islam After Malcolm X*. Doubleday, 1993. 0-385-47011-8

El-Moslimany, Ann P. *Zaki's Ramadan Fast*. Amica Publishing, 1991. ISBN: 1-884187-08-0

Haley, Alex, and Malik El-Shabazz. *The Autobiography of Malcolm X*. Ballantine Books, 1965. ISBN: 0-345-35068-5

Hutchinson, Haji Uthman. *Invincible Abdullah*. American Trust Publications, 1984. ISBN: 0-89259-121-8

MacDonald, Fiona. *A 16th Century Mosque*. Peter Bedrick Books, 1994. ISBN: 0-87226-310-X

Tahan, Malba. *The Man Who Counted—A Collection of Mathematical Adventures*. W.W. Norton, 1993. ISBN: 0-393-30934-7

Judaism

Prepared by

The San Diego County Rabbinical Association
San Diego, CA

"The world depends on three things:
On Torah, worship and loving deeds."

Pirkei Avot (Chapters of the Ancestors) Chap 1:2

Jerusalem. Western (Wailing) Wall.

BASIC TENETS

God

Judaism assumes, rather than feels the need to prove, the existence of God. Judaism introduced to the world (and still adheres to) the concept of monotheism—the belief in the *one* and only God. Judaism's "Godtalk" is about who God is, what God does and the relationship between God and humankind. God is constant, but people are forever growing and developing. So, each person in each generation must discover God, understand God, describe God, struggle with and relate to God in his/her own way.

Covenant

There is a special bond between God and the Jewish People. God chose the Jewish People for the unique task and responsibility of receiving, learning, living and transmitting God's word and will to the world.

Mission

To be a Jew means to have both a personal and communal mission and purpose in life. Each person, created in the image of God, is to imitate God by striving to achieve holiness, to be God-like each and every moment, with each and every thought, word and deed. To be holy means to have God's power to know, to reason and to remember; to reflect God's capacity for demanding justice and righteousness, for feeling compassion, for acting with grace and mercy, for pursuing peace. Together, all Jews strive for *Tikkun Olam,* the perfecting of the world, under the Sovereignty of God—the time when all the ills and evils that beset the world will be ended, and tranquility, harmony and peace will prevail.

Ethical Monotheism

Judaism's ethical system is based on the *authority* of the *Author.* God, who created humankind, has declared how God's children are to behave. God's commandments, called *mitzvot* in Hebrew, are not affected by time or place. They are universal and eternal.

Ritual Observances

In addition to ethical *mitzvot,* God commanded ritual *mitzvot—* rituals, rites and observances which serve to constantly remind us about the mandate for ethical behavior, and which enrich and ennoble daily existence. Rituals that some Jews practice are: daily prayer and recitation of blessings of praise and thanksgiving; the observance of dietary laws; ceremonial observances for life-cycle events, including birth, coming of age, marriage and death; holiday and festival observances. The central holiday observance of Jewish life is the Sabbath, which occurs each week from Friday at sundown until Saturday at sundown and is a time of physical relaxation and spiritual rejuvenation, in imitation of God, who rested on the seventh day following the acts of creation. Other Jewish holiday observances include: Rosh Hashanah (the Jewish New Year), Yom Kippur (the Day of Atonement), Sukkot (Tabernacles), Hanukkah, Purim, Pesakh (Passover) and Shavuot (Pentecost).

Peoplehood

As well as being a religious faith community, Judaism is also a *Peoplehood,* for all Jews share a history, a language, a literature, a land, a culture and a future.

QUESTIONS AND ANSWERS

1. What defines affiliation with your religious tradition?

According to traditional sources, one becomes a Jew by being born to a Jewish mother or by converting to Judaism. This is the definition still adhered to by Orthodox and Conservative Jews. In recent years the Reform movement of Judaism has broadened the definition: one becomes a Jew by being born to a Jewish mother and/or a Jewish father, and by having that identity confirmed by the child's participation in Jewish religious rites.

Because Jews are also an ethnic and national group, one does not necessarily need to practice Judaism (Jewish religion) to be a Jew. However, one who is born a Jew and chooses to practice another religion is, for the most part, no longer considered a member of the Jewish community.

2. What are the major holidays of your faith tradition and what does each represent?

- **Shabbat** (the Sabbath) is the most important Jewish holiday. It is a day of rest, prayer and study, which begins at sundown on Friday evening and concludes after sundown on Saturday evening.
- **Rosh Hashanah** marks the beginning of the new Jewish calendar year and a ten-day period of self-scrutiny, the High Holy Days.
- **Yom Kippur,** the Day of Atonement, concludes these ten days of repentance. Each person is judged by God for his/her sins and seeks forgiveness. The day is one of complete fasting for 24 hours.
- **Sukkot,** the Feast of Booths, is a seven or eight day observance (depending on denomination) marking both the wandering of the Israelites through the wilderness and the fall harvest in the land of Israel. Shemini Atzeret is "the Eighth Day of Gathering" of the Sukkot festival.
- **Simkhat Torah,** the Rejoicing of the Teaching, is the final day of Sukkot and marks the never-ending cycle of Torah. The public reading and study of the book of Deuteronomy is concluded and the book of Genesis is begun.
- **Hanukkah,** which means "dedication," refers to the joyous eight-day celebration through which Jews mark the victory of the Maccabees over the armies of Syria in 165 B.C.E. and the subsequent liberation and "rededication" of the Temple in Jerusalem. A legend relates that a small cruse of oil used to rekindle the Temple candelabra lasted for eight days rather than one.

- **Purim**, the Feast of Lots, marks the deliverance from destruction of the Jews of ancient Persia at the hands of the villainous Haman. This is achieved through the intercession of Esther and Mordecai.
- **Pesach**, or Passover, is the seven or eight day (depending on denomination) spring festival commemorating the Hebrew slaves' exodus from Egypt more than 3,000 years ago. It also marks the beginning of the spring harvest.
- **Yom Ha-Shoah**, the Day of Holocaust Remembrance, is held in memory of those six million or more Jews who were destroyed by the Nazis in World War II.
- **Yom Ha-Atzmaut**, Israel Independence Day, marks the declaration of the independent status of Israel in 1948.
- **Shavuot**, the Feast of Weeks, is the one or two day commemoration (depending on denomination) of the conclusion of the spring harvest and the beginning of the summer harvest. It also is historically linked with the giving of the Torah to the Israelites at Mount Sinai.

3. What are the rituals of your tradition that surround the rites of passage?

- **Birth:** *Brit Milah*—the covenant of circumcision for the boy on the eighth day after birth. *Brit Ha-Branot*—the covenant ceremony for the girl after birth.
- **Education:** *Hanukat Ha-Banim/Ha-Banot*—the boy or girl begins his/her religious studies at about five years of age.
- **Bar/Bat Mitzvah:** Literally, *son/daughter of the Commandment*—special ceremony celebrating the attainment of the age of thirteen, when the boy or girl becomes responsible for the performance of the "mitzvot" (commandments).
- **Marriage:** *Kiddushin/Erusin* and *Nissuin*—According to Talmudic/Rabbinic tradition, these are the two parts of the marriage ritual. The first, *Kiddushin/Erusin,* marks the betrothal and involves an exchange of rings. *Nissuin* is the actual ritual of the marriage ceremony to be performed under the *huppah,* the "marriage canopy." Today these two steps are often combined into one ritual.

- **Divorce:** *Gittin*—Since biblical times Judaism recognized and accepted the possibility that a marriage could fail. Orthodox and Conservative Judaism provide a legal ceremony and ritual for the dissolution of a marriage. The Reconstructionist and Reform movements do not observe such a ritual but accept validity of a civil divorce.
- **Death and Mourning:** Judaism teaches that death is a part of life. As death approaches, the Jew prays directly to God to ask forgiveness for any sins he/she has committed. After his/her death the body is treated with utmost respect, prepared for burial within 24 hours, and then focus shifts to comforting the mourners. Judaism frowns upon or forbids the practices of embalming, viewing the deceased or cremation out of respect for the dead and for God, although some of these rites are practiced by Jews. *Shivah* is a Hebrew word meaning "seven" and refers to a seven-day period of formal mourning by the immediate family of the deceased, beginning immediately after the burial. It is customary to visit the mourners during this time and to provide food and consolation to them. The *Kaddish,* a prayer sanctifying the name of God, is recited by the mourners each day. *Shelosh* is a Hebrew word meaning "thirty" and refers to the traditional thirty-day period of mourning following burial. During this time the mourners avoid parties and all social occasions. At the end of the thirty days, the mourners may return to their regular routine. Thereafter, the death of the relative is observed with the *Yahrzeit,* the annual commemoration of a loved one's death. Many Jews mark this by kindling a "Yahrzeit candle" at home and by reciting the Kaddish prayer at the synagogue.

4. Does your tradition have a view of afterlife? If so, describe it briefly.

There is a wide spectrum of Jewish views relating to life after death. They include:

- **The Biblical View:** In the Torah (the first five books of the Bible) and in the Hebrew Bible in general, there is virtually no intimation of a belief in a heaven or hell, or in physical resurrection. Instead, the biblical idea is that the good will be rewarded and the evil punished in *this* life, rather than in some hereafter.

- **In Second Temple Times:** About the fifth century B.C.E., a new notion began to gain credence in light of the problem of the good suffering and the evil prospering. Jews embraced the idea of life after death and physical resurrection. There would come a day when a Messiah (not a deity) would come and God would raise the dead. At that time, the Jews would be restored to the Land of Israel, where a descendant of the House of David would sit on the throne in a world of peace. The performance of good or evil would be duly compensated in this next world.
- **In the Talmud:** In Talmudic times (500 B.C.E.–500 C.E.), the Second Temple belief had grown into an elaborated system of physical resurrection and immortality of the soul. The Messiah would bring a perfect world.
- **Contemporary Answers:** After the Enlightenment of the eighteenth century, many Jews rejected all notions of a single Messiah, of bodily resurrection and of a physical life after death. Instead, many Jews embraced a belief in the advent of a "Messianic Era." This belief holds that we are co-partners with God in creating a heaven on Earth. Further, our true immortality resides in the memories treasured in this world by those who knew and loved us, or those we influenced through our lives.

Today, all of these views of afterlife exist within the Jewish community.

5. What are the regular personal obligations and worship patterns of your faith's community?

- **Orthodox and Conservative Judaism** hold that one's personal religious and social obligations are determined by *Halacha* (Jewish Law). These rules and regulations were revealed by God to Moses and the Israelite people at Mount

Sinai, and have been subsequently transmitted to future generations in a variety of written and "mundane" activities such as how one washes one's hands before eating. Such regulation is meant to insure the Jew's constant cognizance of God's presence and commanding power in his/her life.

- **Reform and Reconstructionist Judaism** holds that Jewish law was our ancestors' way of determining God's will. However, because these were human interpretations as opposed to Divine commands, they may be accepted or rejected depending upon one's conscience. Nevertheless, some social obligations are still believed to be universal (e.g., the laws against murder) and binding.

- **Traditional Jews** pray three times a day. The pinnacle of the Jewish week is the *Shabbat* (Sabbath), which begins Friday at sunset and concludes Saturday after sunset. This is the day upon which Jews are most likely to attend religious services, which include worship and study of the *Torah* (The Five Books of Moses, the first part of the Hebrew Bible).

6. What are your religion's views about revelation and the source(s) of religious authority?

There are many legitimate responses to this question:

- **Orthodox Judaism** holds that the will of God was revealed at Mt. Sinai in a written and oral form. These forms have been discussed and passed down through the centuries. Because they are the exact word of God, their teachings are still binding on Jews today. The revealed Written and Oral Law, as interpreted by Orthodox rabbis, is the source of religious authority.

- **Conservative Judaism** holds that while God continues to be self-revealing, the records of such revelations are human and thus subject to error. Therefore, the record of these Divine encounters must be taken seriously, but because they are human, the teachings they contain can be interpreted or modified using established procedures. The revealed Written and Oral Law, as interpreted and modified by Conservative rabbis, is the source of religious authority.

- **Reform Judaism** holds that God is revealed to us through the study of the Hebrew Bible, later Jewish writings, the use of human reason and moral striving. Each individual can be the recipient of revelation by observing and participating in the universe, and from this deduce what God required from him/her. Religious authority rests with the individual Jew in his/her ongoing dialogue with God, who is revealed in the world and Jewish tradition.
- **Reconstructionist Judaism** asserts that "God is the power in the universe that makes for salvation." For Reconstructionists, religious authority rests in the individual as he/she participates in the Jewish community.

7. What is your faith's view about salvation?

The term "salvation" is not normally used in Jewish thought; rather Jews speak of "redemption." Because Jews do not believe that we are "born in sin," we therefore hold that we do not require "salvation" or saving from death or punishment. The focus of Jewish thought is not on the afterlife. The emphasis is placed on redeeming the world or ourselves from those things that destroy the values of human existence. Thus, our goal is to work as God's co-partners in triumphing over evil and advancing the social good.

GLOSSARY OF TERMS

Ashkenazim. Jews whose ancestors lived in Eastern Europe.

Bar/Bat Mitzvah. Age at which a boy or girl becomes responsible for observing Jewish tradition on his/her own; 13 for a boy, 12 or 13 for a girl.

B'rit Milah or B'ris. Covenant of Circumcision. Performed on eighth day after birth. Custom goes back to Abraham in the Bible.

Cantor. Clergyperson who leads the congregation in prayer.

Challah. Special braided egg bread served on the Sabbath and other festive occasions.

Dreidel. Spinning top used in Chanukah games.

Haggadah. Special book which contains the Passover story and home rituals.

Hamentaschen. Triangular cookies eaten on Purim.

Hanukkah (Chanukah). Eight-day celebration commemorating the triumph of the Maccabees over the Syrian-Greeks.

Huppah. Wedding canopy.

Kaddish. Prayer which glorifies God. Recited by mourners and during worship services.

Kashrut. Jewish dietary laws.

Kiddush. Blessing over wine on Sabbath, holidays and special occasions.

Kippah or Yarmulke. Simple head covering worn as a sign of respect before God.

Kol Nidre. Opening prayer on Yom Kippur.

Kosher. Something which is fit to eat according to Jewish dietary laws.

Latke. Potato pancake eaten on Hanukkah.

Matzah. Unleavened bread eaten on Passover.

Menorah. Eight-branched candelabrum used on Hanukkah. Seven-branched candelabrum often used in synagogue art.

Mezzuza. Parchment scroll with Biblical quotations affixed to doorpost of home, usually in decorative case. Reminds Jew of God's presence and commandments.

Mitzvah. Religious Commandment. Sometimes used colloquially to mean "good deed."

Mohel. Specially trained person who performs ritual circumcision.

Passover. Holiday commemorating Biblical exodus from Egypt and the beginning of spring harvest.

Purim. Holiday celebrating victory of Jews over their enemies in ancient Persia.

Rabbi. Jewish clergyperson whose primary function is teacher, but also serves as spiritual leader.

Rosh Hashana. Jewish New Year.

Sephardim. Jews whose ancestors lived in Spain or Portugal.

Sabbath or Shabbat or Shabbes. The day of rest, which begins at sundown on Friday and concludes at sundown on Saturday.

Shavuot. Holiday commemorating giving of Torah on Mt. Sinai and the spring harvest festival.

Shema. Central prayer of Judaism; it proclaims uniqueness and unity of God.

Shiva. Seven-day mourning period.

Shofar. Ram's horn sounded on Rosh Hashana.

Simcha. A joyous occasion.

Sukkah. Outdoor temporary hut Jews live in during Sukkot.

Sukkot. Holiday which commemorates the wandering of Israelites in the desert after exodus from Egypt and the fall harvest festival.

Synagogue. House of worship and gathering.

Tallit. Prayer shawl.

Talmud. Compilation of Rabbinic teachings, Biblical interpretations and law.

Tefillin. Leather boxes containing Biblical verses worn during morning prayer.

Torah. Five books of Moses.

Treif. Non-kosher.

Tzedakah. Charity.

Yahrzeit. Anniversary of the date of death.

Yeshiva. A school for intense, traditional Jewish study.

Yom Kippur. Day of Atonement.

SUGGESTED READING

Donin, Hayim Halevy. *To Be a Jew: A Guide to Jewish Observance in Contemporary Life.* Basic Books, 1972.

Eban, Abba. *My Country: The Story of Modern Israel.* Random House, 1972.

Kertzer, Morris N. and Lawrence A. Hoffman. *What is a Jew?* Macmillan Publishing, 1993.

Kushner, Harold S. *To Life!: A Celebration of Jewish Being and Thinking.* Little, Brown and Company, 1993.

Prager, Dennis, and Joseph Telushkin. *Eight Questions People Ask About Judaism.* Tze Ulman, 1985.

Raphael, Marc Lee. *Profiles in American Judaism: The Reform, Conservative, Orthodox and Reconstructionist Traditions in Historical Perspective.* Harper and Row, 1984.

Sacher, Howard M. *The Course of Modern Jewish History.* Dell, 1958.

Seltzer, Robert M. *Jewish People, Jewish Thought: The Jewish Experience in History.* Macmillan Publishing, 1980.

Strassfeld, Michael, Sharon Strassfeld, and Richard Siegal. *The Jewish Catalog: A Do-It-Yourself Kit.* Jewish Publications Society, 1973.

Syme, Daniel B. *The Jewish Home: A Guide for Jewish Living.* Union of American Hebrew Congregations, 1988.

Volakova, Hana. *I Never Saw Another Butterfly: Children's Drawings and Poems from Terezin Concentration Camp, 1942-1944.* Schocken Books, 1978.